SEARCHING THE PAST FOR THE NEW AGE

"The surest way not to fail is to determine to succeed."

—Richard Sheridan (Day 10)

"Don't believe what your eyes are telling you. All they show is limitation."

—Richard Bach,
Jonathan Livingston Seagull (Day 21)

"A man in armor is his armor's slave."

—Robert Browning (Day 93)

"A man is rich in proportion to the number of things which he can afford to let alone."

—Henry David Thoreau (Day 264)

"Let us be silent, that we may hear the whispers of the gods."

—Ralph Waldo Emerson (Day 322)

With the profound writings and inspirational thoughts of such bestselling authors as M. Scott Peck, Marilyn Ferguson, Lao Tzu, and Shakti Gawain, as well as earlier thinkers such as Plato, and Emerson, this unique compendium offers a year's worth of day-by-day selections of the wise and stimulating truths that make up . . .

MEDITATIONS
FOR
THE NEW AGE

MEDITATIONS
FOR
THE NEW AGE

edited by
Carol Tonsing

A SIGNET BOOK

NEW AMERICAN LIBRARY

SIGNET, SIGNET CLASSIC, MENTOR, ONYX, PLUME, MERIDIAN
and NAL BOOKS are published by NAL PENGUIN INC.,
1633 Broadway, New York, New York 10019

First Printing, March, 1989

1 2 3 4 5 6 7 8 9

PRINTED IN THE UNITED STATES OF AMERICA

Introduction

In compiling inspirational insights for the New Age, one cannot help but be struck by how, as Mark Twain put it, "the ancients have stolen our best ideas," by how much the New Age is a time of remembering.

- Remembering when science and mysticism were one, and realizing that both were born of the same sense of wonder, of asking the same questions. Each fed the other, yet for so many years we pretended they were separate. Now, in the full cycle that is happening today, we find them drawing close again, nurturing and reinforcing each other once more.
- Remembering and learning from the ancient cultures who healed themselves and each other using hands, hearts, and tools of the earth. We have long known of the mind's power to heal and to create the atmosphere for health and happiness. Now we are encouraged to take responsibility for every aspect of our lives using our minds as our most powerful helper.
- Remembering that our limits do not stop at our physical bodies. Properly focused, our minds can travel to other dimensions and realities, perhaps other times, places, and lives.

But most urgent for our future, the New Age is a time of remembering when the Earth, which lends us the elements of our physical bodies, was returned our love, respect, and nurturing. Our survival may well depend on our reconnecting with each other and reestablishing our links with the balance of nature.

And so this book becomes a mixture of new insights and their roots in eternal wisdom to remind you each day of the interrelationship of all life, of all times.

MEDITATIONS
FOR
THE NEW AGE

DAY 1

Our crises show us the ways in which our institutions have betrayed nature. We have equated the good life with material consumption, we have dehumanized work and made it needlessly competitive, we are uneasy about our capacities for learning and teaching. Wildly expensive medical care has made little advance against chronic and catastrophic illness while becoming steadily more impersonal, more intrusive. Our government is complex and unresponsive, our social support system is breaking at every stress point.

The potential for rescue at this time of crisis is neither luck, coincidence, nor wishful thinking. Armed with a more sophisticated understanding of how change occurs, we know that the very forces that have brought us to planetary brinksmanship carry in them the seeds of renewal. The current disequilibrium—personal and social—foreshadows a new kind of society. Roles, relationships, institutions and old ideas are being reexamined, reformulated, redesigned.

For the first time in history, humankind has come upon the control panel of change—an understanding of how transformation occurs. We are living in *the change of change*, the time in which we can intentionally align ourselves with nature for rapid remaking of ourselves and our collapsing institutions.

—MARILYN FERGUSON
The Aquarian Conspiracy

DAY 2

There are many paths available for seeking the light within. To start, you have to recognize that there is something precious within to be found, in spite of our culture's pressure to keep us externally oriented, looking for happiness by being consumers of external goods. You have to continually struggle against the social current, of course; people who go within are dangerous and unpredictable, so society distrusts, discourages and often punishes them. . . .

All genuine paths require courage: courage to buck the social tide, courage to see yourself as you really are, courage to take risks. Progress on any genuine path is a gift to us all, as well as a gain for yourself.

—CHARLES TART
Waking Up

DAY 3

The proper study of mankind is man.

—PLATO

DAY 4

Life appears unwilling merely to make itself at home in the material universe; determined rather to use that material universe in its persistent and creative effort towards the discovery or acquirement of something else, of a new kind of reality over against all mere nature.

—EVELYN UNDERHILL
The Mystic Way

DAY 5

The lips of wisdom are closed, except to the ears of understanding.

—THE KYBALION

DAY 6

In our somewhat clinical, and some would say alienating, modern society, access to the sacred and awesome areas of being is harder to come by. Some have found this type of mystical experience through a church, others through meditation or through psychedelic states of consciousness. It seems to me that one should refrain from passing judgment on whether one path is superior to or more appropriate than another. In the final analysis we are all seeking a personal mythology, a framework of meaning which encompasses not only the complex realities of modern life but also the abstract and intangible realms of our inner being.

The path to the sacred introduces us to profound areas of meaning. We begin to understand our place within the cyclical and universal processes of Nature and—perhaps for the first time —we are able to participate in the mythologies that have enriched our culture centuries before we were born.

—NEVILL DRURY
Visionquest

DAY 7

All truths are old, and all that we have to do is recognize and utter them anew.

—GOETHE

DAY 8

Let a man learn to look for the permanent in the mutable and fleeting; let him learn to bear the disappearance of things he was wont to reverence without losing his reverence; let him learn that he is here not to work, but to be worked upon; and that, though abyss open under abyss, and opinion displace opinion, all are at last contained in the Eternal Cause.

—EMERSON

DAY 9

First say to yourself what you would be; and then do what you have to do.

—EPICTETUS

DAY 10

The surest way not to fail is to determine to succeed.

—RICHARD BRINSLEY SHERIDAN

DAY 11

The scientist works on matter and needs proof
The saint works with meditation and by prayer
Therefore the medium works with the grey area
Each works with his own kind of conscience.

The three work for the good of humanity and the future.
(They do not work for the past.)
We are penetrating into a new era of evolution which joins science and spirituality.
It is the dawn of a new day whose rays give us a message and reality built on perception, intuition and healing.

The choice which we make and the way we utilize our energy can enhance the great evolution or the destruction of humanity. We are on the frontier of a new age, the last frontier, the frontier of the spirit.

—ALEX TANNOUS
Reflexions sur la Vie Interieure

DAY 12

Your soul is here to perceive past the limitations of your five senses, past the limitations of the immediate world around you. Something else is impinging on you. Something else is pushing you. You are all multidimensional beings. You are brilliant light-souls who have a frame of reference for being out of body, for being in light body, for knowing all things. In fact, you have the capacity within your very being to heal yourselves, to heal each other, to perform miracles.

—CHRIS GRISCOM
Ecstacy Is a New Frequency

DAY 13

I know of no more encouraging fact than the unquestionable ability of man to elevate his life by a conscious endeavor.

—THOREAU

DAY 14

I suppose none of us doubts that there is such a thing as the power of suggestion and that it can produce very great results indeed, and that it is par excellence a hidden power; it works behind the scenes, it works through what we know as the subconscious mind, and consequently its activity is not immediately recognizable, or the source from which it comes. . . . In itself it is perfectly neutral, it all depends on the purpose for which it is used, and the character of the agent who employs it.

—THOMAS TROWARD
The Hidden Power

DAY 15

Remember that all things are only opinion and that it is in your power to think as you please.

—MARCUS AURELIUS

DAY 16

Your life is your process, and when you love it you love yourself. You have a much larger vision of yourself and what is important in your growth.

—SHARON C. BROWN, PAT A. PAULSON, AND JO ANN WOLF
Living on Purpose

DAY 17

I was drafted by my Goddess.

I thought I would grow up to be a journalist, an actress, a dancer—a beauty queen. Instead, I find that all my acquired skills were grooming me to become a teacher, a healer, a servant of the Mother of Beauty. Looking at the situation in retrospect, I realize that She took good care with my education. She edited out the garbage and rewrote the script. She lured me into experiences, prompted me to formulate new words and reconsider the definitions of old ones. She made sure I met the right people, in the right places, at the right time.

And she saw to it that I was in the right frame of mind to respond accordingly to the offering laid before me. This is, in my opinion, the essence of *luck*.

—LUISAH TEISH
Jambalaya: The Natural Woman's Book of Personal Charms and Practical Rituals

DAY 18

Always think of what you have to do as easy and it will be.

—EMILE COUE
*Self-Mastery through
Conscious Auto-suggestion*

DAY 19

The way to use life is to do nothing through acting,
The way to use life is to do everything through being.
When a leader knows this,
His land naturally goes straight.
And the world's passion to stray from straightness
Is checked at the core
By the simple unnameable cleanness
Through which men cease from coveting,
And to a land where men cease from coveting
Peace comes of course.

—LAO TZU

DAY 20

The secrets of existence are only accessible to an extent corresponding to man's own degree of maturity. For this reason alone the path to the higher stages of knowledge and power is beset with obstacles. A firearm should not be used until sufficient experience has been gained to avoid disaster caused by its use.

—RUDOLF STEINER

DAY 21

Don't believe what your eyes are telling you. All they show is limitation. Look with your understanding, find out what you already know, and you'll see the way to fly.

—RICHARD BACH
Jonathan Livingston Seagull

DAY 22

To me every hour of the light and dark is a miracle.
Every inch of space is a miracle.

—WALT WHITMAN

DAY 23

All we are dealing with wherever we live in the Universe is just different levels of energy, some of which is unmanifest at one extreme, called spirit, and some of which we find at the other extreme in a manifest form which we call matter. Because it is ALL energy and all energy obeys a few basic laws. They are called the laws of physics in science, and called spiritual law in esoterics—everything in the Universe obeys *exactly the same laws*. The way we see and experience them simply depends on our perspective.

What you see, depends on where you stand.

—RA BONEWITZ
The Cosmic Crystal Spiral

DAY 24

Before you can do something, you must first be something.

—GOETHE

DAY 25

Change your thoughts and you change your world.

—NORMAN VINCENT PEALE

DAY 26

Metaphysics consists of two parts: first, that which all men of sense already know, and second, that which they can never know.

—VOLTAIRE

DAY 27

I see science and mysticism as two complementary manifestations of the human mind: of its rational and intuitive faculties. The modern physicist experiences the world through an extreme specialization of the rational mind; the mystic through an extreme specialization of the intuitive mind. The two approaches are entirely different and involve far more than a certain view of the physical world. However, they are complementary as we have learned to say in physics. Neither is comprehended in the other, nor can either of them be reduced to the other; but both are necessary, supplementing one another for a fuller understanding of the world. To paraphrase an old Chinese saying, mystics understand the roots of the Tao but not its branches; scientists understand its branches but not its roots. Science does not need mysticism and mysticism does not need science, but men and women need both. Mystical experience is necessary to understand the deepest nature of things, and science is essential for modern life. What we need, therefore, is not a synthesis, but a dynamic interplay between mystical intuition and scientific analysis.

—FRITJOF CAPRA
The Tao of Physics

DAY 28

It is the fragmented mind which does not see the thing as it is.

—PATANJALI
Yoga Sutras

DAY 29

We turn to Spirit for help when our foundations
are shaking, only to find out that it is Spirit who
is shaking them.

—DAN MILLMAN
The Way of the Peaceful Warrior

DAY 30

Letting go of our suffering is the hardest work we will ever do. It is also the most fruitful. To heal means to meet ourselves in a new way—in the newness of each moment where all is possible and nothing is limited to the old, our holding released, our grasping seen with little surprise or judgment. The vastness of our being meeting each moment wholeheartedly whether it holds pleasure or pain. Then the healing goes deeper than we ever imagined, deeper than we ever dreamed.

—STEPHEN LEVINE
Healing into Life and Death

DAY 31

We keep so busy talking
we are so keen to act
that we forget
that in the heart
lies all we need
untapped, intact.

—ANGELUS SILESIUS
The Book of Angelus Silesius

DAY 32

When you first receive a crystal, no matter how you get it, whether it is given to you, purchased or found, take it into meditation with you and meditate on the reasons why it has come to you. Ask the crystal what uses it is in harmony with and what it would like to be used for. The response may be an intuitive feeling, a vision or a particular use, or even a sense of a verbal reply. Just leave your mind open to whatever happens as you contact the living intelligence behind the physical form, the essence or elemental energy of the crystal.

—KORRA DEAVER
Rock Crystal, The Magic Stone

DAY 33

Every day, in every way, I'm getting better and better.

—EMILE COUE
*Self-Mastery through
Conscious Auto-suggestion*

DAY 34

Most meditation teachers recommend beginning by using some simple object as an aid, but the important thing to remember is that it is not the particular object or technique that matters. What's important is the process of bringing one's mind back to its object of focus when it wanders. It's important to do this gently and without judgment, by the way. Meditation takes effort, but it is not a war. It is a way of making friends with yourself.

—RICK FIELDS
Chop Wood, Carry Water

DAY 35

No expert, authority or sage knows *you* as well as you know yourself. When it comes to your inner world and the things that affect it, you are the authority. You are the expert. You are the god of your microcosmos, and you must take the responsibility for ordering it.

—GREG NIELSEN AND JOSEPH POLANSKY
Pendulum Power

DAY 36

True individuality is never needlessly aggressive; it never demands that others should conform to it; but it is manly, womanly, courageous enough to establish good principles rather than follow bad fashions.

—W. J. COLVILLE
in *The Metaphysical Magazine*, 1895

DAY 37

Many mansions are in that body, many temples. For the body has been again and again in the experience of the earth; they are sometimes mansions, sometimes homes, sometimes huts.

Know that in whatever state you find yourself —of mind, of body, of physical condition—that is what you have built and is necessary for your unfoldment.

Know that in whatever state you find yourself, that, at the moment is best for you. Do not look back upon what might have been. Rather lift up, look up, now, where you are.

—EDGAR CAYCE

DAY 38

You cannot teach a man anything. You can only help him to find it within himself.

—GALILEO

DAY 39

If you want to do a certain thing,
you first have to be a certain person.
Once you have become that certain person,
you will not care anymore about doing that
  certain thing.

—DOGEN

DAY 40

We both exist and know that we exist, and rejoice in this knowledge.

—SAINT AUGUSTINE

DAY 41

The deepest level of listening is silence. The center of all sound is silence. All sounds rise from and lead back to silence. Listening is the art of discovering silence. Silence is the key to the many adventures the world of sound has to offer. Through silence we are truly safe and free. We know the beginning and we know the end.

—JOHN BEAULIEU
Music and Sound in the Healing Arts

DAY 42

In the complete cessation of thought comes the precious gift of spiritual illumination.

—PATANJALI
Yoga Sutras

DAY 43

Properly chosen sounds can actually help bring you into a greater degree of physical and psychological harmony and balance.

Perhaps the most important element in choosing healthy sound is knowing what feels right and works for you. Of course, what is music to your ears may be annoying to a neighbor, or even to another family member. Like taste in food, taste in sound differs with individuals. . . .

In order to focus consciously on the sounds that your body is ingesting, sit quietly for at least five minutes and make a list of each different sound that you hear. Next to each sound on your list put a *W* (for a welcome sound) or a *U* (for an unwelcome sound). You'll be surprised by what you discover.

—STEVE HALPERN WITH LOUIS SAVERY
Sound Health

DAY 44

Shamans in South America typically believe that one is not able to enter the world of the spirit until one can suppress the "chatter" that continually goes on inside the brain. This "inner-brain chatter," whether it be a dialogue or a song rambling through our minds, preserves through words and music the reality that we learned in our homes and schools and that defines the limits of human capabilities. Shamans believe that we live as prisoners of a cultural trance, blindly inhabiting a small corner of the universe of possibilities. . . .

This is a point of view that closely resembles the model of reality held by the physics of quantum mechanics. Quantum Theory can be interpreted to state that our material world is created again and again before our eyes in the eyes of the beholder, in the act of beholding itself. The shaman takes this one step further, believing that if you can change your perception of reality, you can actually influence events in the material world. Thus if one can change one's perception of illness, one can influence and accelerate the ordinary course of healing. If one can change one's perception of a neighboring tribe, one can bring about peace with that tribe. Thus reality, from the point of view of the shaman, emerges from an individual's or society's expectations.

—ALBERTO VILLODO AND STANLEY KRIPPNER
Healing States

DAY 45

To change your mood or mental state—change your vibration.

One may change his mental vibrations by an effort of Will, in the direction of deliberately fixing the Attention upon a more desirable state. Will directs the Attention and Attention changes the Vibration. Cultivate the Art of Attention, by means of the Will, and you have solved the secret of the Mastery of Moods and Mental States.

—THE KYBALION

DAY 46

Our feet are our channels of communication with the earth, and they hold one of the keys to the healing and energizing forces within us. We allow our fingers to work on the feet, to go where they will, to explore, probe, vibrate and rub. We acknowledge the higher wisdom of the life force to bring about the changes we need. All we do is loosen a time structure. If a gutter pipe is blocked with leaves, it is no good pushing and bashing at it. The easiest way is for water to be poured through and for the pipe to be gently shaken. The blockage will move. So life moves without force. As long as there is life, our potential to flow freely can be realized.

If we have attracted to ourselves certain characteristics, why do we want to change them? We do it so we may see the deeper purpose beyond. We have the choice of losing what we think we are and finding ourselves beyond the influences that have created the fabric of our self. We have the choice between being stuck with our view of life or opening new vistas within ourselves so we may see beyond. Nothing is permanent, nothing is fixed, so it is up to us to take the responsibility for our own evolution and begin to reach beyond our limitations. Our potential is limitless and the choice is ours. However, the ultimate choice is up to life, and we are that life.

—GASTON ST. PIERRE AND DEBBIE BOATER
The Metamorphic Technique

DAY 47

It is not death that a man should fear, but he should fear never beginning to live.

—MARCUS AURELIUS

DAY 48

Far better it is to dare mighty things, to win glorious triumphs, even though checkered by failure, than to take rank with those poor spirits who neither enjoy much nor suffer much, because they live in the gray twilight that knows not victory or defeat.

The joy of living is his who has the heart to demand it.

—THEODORE ROOSEVELT

DAY 49

Public opinion is a weak tyrant compared with our own private opinion. What a man thinks of himself, that is which determines, or rather, indicates, his fate.

—THOREAU

DAY 50

One's distance from Heaven is in proportion to the measure of one's self-love.

—EMANUEL SWEDENBORG

DAY 51

Good suggestions, of whatever character they may be or to whomsoever they may be addressed, invariably react upon the character of the suggester. It is impossible for one to suggest moral principles to another without being morally benefited himself. . . . As the teacher is benefited by fixing the lesson taught more firmly in his own mind, so is a suggestion, moral or therapeutical, beneficial to him who makes it. Like the quality of mercy, "It is twice blessed; it blesseth him that gives and him that takes."

—THOMSON JAY HUDSON
The Law of Mental Medicine

DAY 52

The things which are given to you on earth are given you purely as an exercise, a "blank sheet" on which you make your own mind and heart. . . . It matters very little what becomes of the fruits of the earth, or what they are worth. The whole question is whether you have used them in order to learn how to obey and how to love.

—PIERRE TEILHARD DE CHARDIN
The Divine Milieu

DAY 53

I must create a system, or be enslaved by another man's.

—WILLIAM BLAKE

DAY 54

People are usually more convinced by reasons they discovered themselves than by those found by others.

—PASCAL

DAY 55

All dream images are parts of ourselves that we have disowned because we find them a threat to the conscious image we have of ourselves. So we push them outside our "ego boundary," the sphere of conscious awareness, and say, "That's not me." Many people in our culture disown the weak, vulnerable side of themselves, which they consider "unmanly," while others push away the aggressive and sexual aspects of their personality because they are supposed to be "unchristian." But although the ego repudiates these unwanted qualities, they still remain within our total psychic states and are part of us. . . .

One simple test to discover the disowned aspects of ourselves is to ask what we hate most of all in other people, for we are almost sure to find the very same thing simmering away in ourselves below the level of conscious awareness, just waiting for an opportunity to express itself.

—DR. ANN FARADAY
Dream Power

DAY 56

The wise man falls in with the Law, and by understanding its movements he operates it instead of being its blind slave. Just as does the skilled swimmer turn this way and that way, going and coming as he will, instead of being as the log which is carried here and there—so is the wise man as compared to the ordinary man, and yet both swimmer and log, wise man and fool, are subject to Law. He who understand this is well on the road to Mastery.

—THE KYBALION

DAY 57

To have compassion for yourself is vital. Self-observation in its various forms eventually leads to a depth of understanding we seldom dream of. A vital part of that understanding will be how pure and marvelous you essentially are. There will be resistance to self-understanding on the way as you see negative parts of yourself, but the process is worth it.

Until you learn to understand and have compassion toward yourself, all your tolerance, love and compassion toward others rests on a very shaky foundation.

—CHARLES TART
Waking Up

DAY 58

No man is happy who does not think himself so.

—PUBLIUS SYRUS

DAY 59

Root to root we stand
The trees and I
They, with their feet
reaching downward
rich, moist, warm soil.
Earth-bound are we.
One, with the desire
to be free
of the
confines of
Breath.

—OH SHINNAH
in *Five Great Healers Speak Here*

DAY 60

Alas! The fearful Unbelief is unbelief in yourself.

—THOMAS CARLYLE

DAY 61

You can create opportunity for yourself by speaking about your Life Work as you want it to be. All of your life counts, and you don't know where or when the most important opportunity will show up. You create the significance of your Life Work. Start today telling your Life Work in the largest way you can think of. Let yourself dream about and envision the impact you want your Life Work to make. How can you make a difference in the life of your work? What do you believe needs to happen about it that would give you great joy? If nothing stopped you, what and how would you live your life? Life Work is a big idea. You get fulfillment and passion when you talk into life the big idea of your Life Work.

—SHARON C. BROWN, PAT A. PAULSON, AND
    JO ANN WOLF
    Living on Purpose

DAY 62

Much of man's unhappiness is caused, first, by self-ignorance and, second, by self-concealment.

—DR. ANN FARADAY
Dream Power

DAY 63

Of all the beautiful truths pertaining to the soul which have been restored and brought to light in this age, none is more gladdening or fruitful of divine promise and confidence than this—that you are the master of your thought, the molder of your character, and the maker and shaper of your condition, environment, and destiny.

—JAMES ALLEN
As You Think

DAY 64

They can because they think they can.

—VIRGIL

DAY 65

Most of us are like little children or young adolescents; we believe that the freedom and power of adulthood is our due, but we have little taste for adult responsibility and self-discipline. Much as we feel oppressed by our parents—or by society or fate—we actually seem to need to have powers above us to blame for our condition. To rise to a position of such power that we have no one except ourselves is a fearful state of affairs. . . . Were it not for God's presence within us in that exalted position, we would be terrified by our aloneness. Still, many have so little capacity to tolerate the aloneness of power that they reject God's presence, rather than experience themselves as the sole master of their ship. Most people want peace without the aloneness of power. And they want the self-confidence of adulthood without having to grow up.

—M. SCOTT PECK
The Road Less Traveled

DAY 66

What the entity is today is the result of what it has been in days and experiences and ages and aeons past. For life is continuous; and whether it is manifested in materiality or in other realms of consciousness, it is one and the same.

—EDGAR CAYCE

DAY 67

The love and peace of higher consciousness flow from just being—and enjoying it all. Anything you do will not be enough unless you feel fulfilled in just being. Usually we are not happy when we find doing whatever it is that we think we have to do. Doing creates expectations that your world and the people around you may or may not fit. The things we do disappear in time. We must learn to appreciate just being alive in the nowness of whatever situation we are in.

—KEN KEYES, JR.
Handbook to Higher Consciousness

DAY 68

In nature, there can never be two things which are exactly alike.

—LEIBNITZ

DAY 69

A Master teaches essence. When the essence is perceived, he teaches what is necessary to expand the perception. The Wu Li Master does not speak of gravity until the student stands in wonder at the flower petal falling to the ground. He does not speak of laws until the student, of his own, says, "How strange, I drop two stones simultaneously, one heavy and one light, and *both* of them reach the earth at the same moment!" He does not speak of mathematics until the student says, "There must be a way to express this more simply."

In this way, the Wu Li Master dances with his student. The Wu Li Master does not teach, but the student learns. The Wu Li Master always begins at the center, at the heart of the matter.

—GARY ZUKAV
The Dancing Wu Li Masters

DAY 70

Mind is held to be of all phenomena the most supernatural.

—ARISTOTLE

DAY 71

Beingness, doingness and havingness are like a triangle where each side supports the others.

They are not in conflict with each other.
They each exist simultaneously.

Often people attempt to live their lives backwards. They try to *have* things, or more money, in order to *do* more of what they want, so that they will be happier.

The way it works is the reverse. You must first *be* who you really are, then *do* what you need to do, in order to *have* what you want.

—SHAKTI GAWAIN
Creative Visualization

DAY 72

Chant for Self-Esteem

(To be recited any time you doubt that you are a powerful person.)
Earth, Water, Fire and Air
Within me all things are there
Flesh on my bones is like the Earth
It's soft, but strong and full of worth
The blood that flows within my veins
Is like the ocean, river, and rain
My spirit soars and takes me higher
Here is where I keep my fire
My breath and thoughts are like the air
I can do everything and go anywhere
Earth, water, fire and air
Within me all things are there
And so I pledge unto myself
Power, love, health and wealth.

—LUISAH TEISH
Jambalaya: The Natural Woman's Book of Personal Charms and Practical Rituals

DAY 73

Your imagination is your preview of life's coming attractions.

—ALBERT EINSTEIN

DAY 74

One who is anciently aware of existence
Is master of every moment,
Feels no break since time beyond time
In the way life flows.

—LAO TZU

DAY 75

Agnes Whistling Elk:
We all come into this earth walk to heal our femaleness. Man or woman, it makes no difference. Women come into this round knowing a great truth. But like most women, you couldn't define what you knew. Some women become indifferent to this knowledge. You wanted to understand this knowledge. . . . When men come into this round, they do not know. If they are lucky, they realize they have to find a woman to teach them. Men do not know how to live. Women must teach them that. But first women have to take their own power and heal themselves. They imitate men like a mockingbird imitates a crow. Once they do that, it's all over. It's all wrong. Men and women both lose and become weak. If you had chosen that man, beautiful as he was, and not your own power, he would have destroyed you. He would have hated you for not being White Buffalo Woman for him to learn from. When you are a goddess, then you can mate with your god successfully, and only then.

—LYNN ANDREWS
Jaguar Woman

DAY 76

One radiant energy pervades and gives rise to all life. While it may speak to us through plants, nature spirits or the human beings with whom we share life on this planet, all are reflections of the deeper reality behind and within them. . . . Essentially, the devas and nature spirits are aspects of our own selves, guiding us toward our true identity, the divine reality within.

—THE FINDHORN COMMUNITY
The Findhorn Garden Book

DAY 77

A metaphysician is a man who goes into a dark cellar at midnight without a light looking for a black cat that is not there.

—BARON BOWEN OF COLWOOD

DAY 78

Faith separate from love is not faith, but mere science, which in itself is void of spiritual life.

—EMANUEL SWEDENBORG

DAY 79

Those who spread their sails in the right way to the winds of the earth will always find themselves borne by a current towards the open seas. The more nobly a man wills and acts, the more avid he becomes for great and sublime aims to pursue. He will no longer be content with family, country and the remunerative aspect of his work. He will want wider organizations to create, new paths to blaze, causes to uphold, truths to discover, an ideal to cherish and defend. So, gradually, the worker no longer belongs to himself. Little by little the great breath of the universe has insinuated itself into him through the fissure of his humble but faithful action, has broadened him, raised him up, borne him on.

—PIERRE TEILHARD DE CHARDIN
The Divine Milieu

DAY 80

Acquisition of [higher] knowledge is not the end, but the means to the end; the end consists of the attainment, thanks to this knowledge of the higher worlds, of greater and truer self-confidence, a higher degree of courage, and a magnanimity and perseverance such as cannot, as a rule, be acquired in the lower world.

—RUDOLF STEINER

DAY 81

A man lives by believing something, not by debating and arguing many things.

—THOMAS CARLYLE

DAY 82

It is better to make a mistake with the full force of your being than to carefully avoid mistakes with a trembling spirit. Responsibility means recognizing both pleasure and price, making a choice based on that recognition, and living with that choice without concern.

—DAN MILLMAN
Way of the Peaceful Warrior

DAY 83

For every one step that you take in the pursuit of higher knowledge, take three steps in the perfection of your own character.

—RUDOLF STEINER

DAY 84

How can you know,
as long as there is a portion of you
that is human,
what is perfect and what is not
Perhaps in the Divine Plan,
which IS perfect, a dusting of human imperfection
is absolutely perfect for the moment.

—EMMANUEL

DAY 85

It is on your own self-knowledge and experience that the knowledge of everything else depends.

—THE CLOUD OF UNKNOWING

DAY 86

Hoping for the best but dreading the worst is the mental attitude of millions who neutralize the good of their hope by the folly of their dread. It is impossible to serve two masters, and no two can be more diametrically opposed than dread and hope. Anticipation of coming trouble brings to pass the very calamities we fear most, for by brooding over a thing we generate the conditions for its ultimation.

—W. J. COLVILLE

DAY 87

Ghost, n. The outward and visible sign of an inward fear.

—AMBROSE BIERCE

DAY 88

You are buffeted by circumstances so long as you believe yourself to be a creature affected by outside conditions—but when you realize that you are a creative power, and that you may command the hidden soil and seeds of your being out of which your circumstances grow, then you become the rightful master of yourself.

—JAMES ALLEN
As You Think

DAY 89

I know well what I am fleeing from but not what I am in search of.

—MONTAIGNE

DAY 90

No one can make you feel inferior without your consent.

—ELEANOR ROOSEVELT

DAY 91

Binding and Breaking Stones

The great binder in life and love is the blue sapphire (Taurus). It bestows fidelity and attachment when given as a love-token to a sweetheart. If someone else takes and wears it they will be bound to the original giver.

Rose quartz gives a younger and warmer love that is not quite so lasting (Venus—Moon).

The ruby gives a glowing love (Aries).

The dark-red garnet gives a more hidden love which is not exuberant but nevertheless deeply passionate. However, it can lead to hate and separation due to its jealous potential (Scorpio).

On the other hand, the flesh-pink carnelian gives and strengthens the solidarity due to love relationships, love of one's own family and an appreciation of the meaning of kindship: it encourages love between parents and children (Virgo).

The amethyst encourages the love and worship of God.

The turquoise enters into the spontaneous upsurge of romantic love and leads to remarkable encounters with people from a past life (Uranus).

Chalcedony is a binder on the mental plane for assisting connected thinking at an impersonal level. It helps in the spinning of a coherent pattern of thoughts.

—MELLIE UYLDERT
The Magic of Precious Stones

DAY 92

And what is life? God manifested in the material plane. For it is still in Him that we live and move and have our being. Life is a material manifestation of that universal force or energy that we call God.

A soul is a portion of the Divine Energy, and is as everlasting as that energy itself. Thus, if there is a continued period of activity that is for self-exaltation, then the entity may be said to be separating itself, or losing its relationship. Those however that worship and glorify the First Cause are mindful of the first command to man, in the expression: "Thou shalt have no other Gods before me"—before the I AM of the soul.

—EDGAR CAYCE

DAY 93

A man in armor is his armor's slave.

—ROBERT BROWNING

DAY 94

Every man takes the limits of his own field of vision for the limits of the world.

—SCHOPENHAUER

DAY 95

Problems are the cutting edge that distinguishes between success and failure. Problems call forth our courage and our wisdom, indeed they create our courage and our wisdom. It is only because of problems that we grow mentally and spiritually. When we desire to encourage the growth of the human spirit, we challenge and encourage the human capacity to solve problems, just as in school we deliberately set problems for our children to solve. It is through the pain of confronting and resolving problems that we learn. . . . It is for this reason that wise people learn not to dread, but actually to welcome problems and actually to welcome the pain of problems.

—M. SCOTT PECK
The Road Less Traveled

DAY 96

Be not afraid of life. Believe that life is worth living, and your belief will help create the fact.

—WILLIAM JAMES

DAY 97

Only those are fit to live who do not fear to die; and none are fit to die who have shrunk from the joy of life and the duty of life. Both life and death are part of the same Great Adventure.

—THEODORE ROOSEVELT

DAY 98

If our habitual conditioning is to overcome our pain, we will have a tendency to feel overwhelmed when things don't go the way we wish. We may even feel a need to "beat" another's pain. We will find it difficult to connect with them just where they are. We won't be able to touch them with love because if we want anything from somebody, even for them to be out of pain, they will be an object in our mind rather than the subject of our heart. If we can open to our own pain and explore our resistances and long-held aversions, there arises the possibility of touching another's pain with compassion, of meeting another as we meet ourselves with a bit more clarity and tenderness. We see in such instances how the work we do on ourselves is clearly of benefit to all sentient beings. Each person who works to open his heart touches the heart of us all. When we are no longer recreating the problem, we reaffirm the solution. We discover from day to day how the healing we do for ourselves is a healing for all.

—STEPHEN LEVINE
Healing into Life and Death

DAY 99

Nature has some perfections to show that she is the image of God, and some defects, to show that she is only His image.

—PASCAL

DAY 100

Whoever knows more than his neighbor is honor bound to show his neighbor the highest light which he himself enjoys. In so doing, two great advantages are at once secured: he who sheds the light is not only a blessing to others, but he himself will enjoy superior health, joy and freedom by asking of the soul within, rather than of the world without, "What wilt thou have me to do?"

—W. J. COLVILLE

DAY 101

You gain strength, courage and confidence by every experience in which you really stop to look fear in the face. You are able to say to yourself, "I lived through this horror. I can take the next thing that comes along." You must do the thing you think you cannot do.

—ELEANOR ROOSEVELT

DAY 102

Exercise: Scrying Through Denial

Fill a dark bowl with water. Create sacred space. Sit comfortably and gaze into the water.

Ask yourself: What do I know that I'm afraid to know? What might I see that I'm afraid to see?

Don't force answers. Let images or thoughts arise, and simply note what they are. When you get tired, open your circle and pour the water out.

Do this over time: nightly for a full season is best.

If disturbing information surfaces, find a supportive group or person with whom you can share. Members of a circle or group could do this meditation throughout the same period of time, and check in with each other about what comes up.

—STARHAWK
Truth or Dare

DAY 103

The only man who makes no mistakes is the man
who never does anything.

—THEODORE ROOSEVELT

DAY 104

Understand the danger in speaking negatively about yourself and others. If you want a great life, one of the things you must do is to think and speak about your life in the most generous terms. Hold it as wonderful, and it will have a shot at being wonderful.

What not to trash: yourself, your significant other, your children, anything you care about. And don't let anyone else trash them either.

—SHARON C. BROWN, PAT A. PAULSON, AND JO ANN WOLF
Living on Purpose

DAY 105

There is nothing either good or bad, but thinking makes it so.

—SHAKESPEARE

DAY 106

In great trials a man generally tries to act as he ought, while in little affairs he shows himself as he really is.

—ANONYMOUS

DAY 107

There is a great deal of support in the world for a negative attitude toward environmental sounds: such sounds are not musical; they are unwanted; they have no beauty; they are dangerous to our health. The collective mind believes these attitudes and empowers them. For instance, we cross a street and see a truck coming. We know the truck is running a red light, but we refuse to get out of the way because of a thought, "The truck has no right to break the law." Our attitude may be right and we may be in the hospital because of it. The same situation exists with mental attitudes about environmental sounds. These sounds are with us, and whether they have a right to be here or not, we cannot avoid them. Children who haven't learned mental attitudes about environmental sounds have a special ability to enjoy them. They love the sounds of tractors, planes, subways, trains, air hammers, creaky doors, etc. We adults also have this ability; we have only to give ourselves permission to listen like a child, permission to forget the important activities of the day and enter into the unavoidable reality of a sound.

—JOHN BEAULIEU
Music and Sound in the Healing Arts

DAY 108

Little things affect little minds.

—BENJAMIN DISRAELI

DAY 109

Nothing on earth consumes a man more quickly than the passion of resentment.

—NIETZSCHE

DAY 110

To prevent contact with the entrapped spirits of darkness, you must practice loving all living things unconditionally and seek to make contact with your Higher Self, your Soul. When you vibrate with the highest form of love, contact with your Soul is quite easy, for both of you are vibrating on a similar frequency.

—BRAD STEIGER
The World Beyond Death

DAY 111

The biggest problem in the world could have been
solved when it was small.

—LAO TZU

DAY 112

There are many ways of behaving when one is in a normal setting, but when one is alone, in danger, in darkness, there is only one way: the warrior's way. . . .

Under the impact of an unfamiliar life situation, I had found out that not to surrender means freedom, that not to feel self-important breeds an indomitable fierceness, and that to vanquish moral judgments brings an all-soothing humbleness that is not servitude.

—FLORINDA DONNER
The Witch's Dream

DAY 113

He that falls in love with himself will have no rivals.

—BENJAMIN FRANKLIN

DAY 114

Life is warning you to get rid of an addiction every time you are emotionally uncomfortable in any way.

—KEN KEYES, JR.
Handbook of Higher Consciousness

DAY 115

Thoughts are things; the mind is as concrete as a post or tree.

Study yourself, for in the self one may find the answer to all the problems that may confront you. For the spirit of man, with all its attributes, physical and mental, is a portion of the whole great spirit. Hence the answers are all within the self. Know this—that all power, all healing, all help must come from within.

—EDGAR CAYCE

DAY 116

Those whom God wishes to destroy, he first makes angry.

—EURIPIDES

DAY 117

The mystics are artists, and the stuff in which they work is most often human life. They want to heal the disharmony between the actual and the real; and since in the white-hot radiance of that faith, hope and charity which burns in them, they discern such a reconciliation to be possible, they are able to work for it with a singleness of purpose and an invincible optimism denied to other men.

—EVELYN UNDERHILL
Practical Mysticism

DAY 118

Thinking about sense-objects
Will attach you to sense-objects;
Grow attached, and you become addicted;
Thwart your addiction, it turns to anger;
Be angry, and you confuse your mind;
Confuse your mind, you forget the lesson of
    experience;
Forget experience, you lose discrimination;
Lose discrimination, and you miss life's only
    purpose.

—BHAGAVAD-GITA

DAY 119

Nature is schoolmistress, the soul the pupil, and whatever one has taught or the other learned has come from God—the Teacher of the teacher.

—TERTULLIAN

DAY 120

To understand a problem obviously requires a certain intelligence, and that intelligence cannot be derived from or cultivated through specialization. It comes into being only when we are passively aware of the whole process of our consciousness, which is to be aware of ourselves without choice, without choosing what is right and what is wrong. When you are passively aware, you will see that out of that passivity—which is not idleness, which is not sleep, but extreme alertness— the problem has quite a different significance; which means there is no longer identification with the problem and therefore there is no judgment and hence the problem begins to reveal its content. If you are able to do that constantly, continuously, then every problem can be solved fundamentally, not superficially.

—KRISHNAMURTI

DAY 121

Threads of meaning bind us to every other thing and to each other. Severing too many of the threads results in the death of the spirit.

Education strays from reality when it divides its knowledge into separate compartments without due regard to the connection between them.

—FRANCES WOSMEK
Acknowledge the Wonder

DAY 122

There slumber in every human being faculties by means of which he can acquire for himself a knowledge of higher worlds. . . . This esoteric knowledge is no more of a secret for the average human being than writing is a secret for those who have never learned it. And just as all can learn to write who choose the correct method, so, too, can all who seek the right way become esoteric students and even teachers. In one respect only do the conditions here differ from those that apply to external knowledge and proficiency. The possibility of acquiring the art of writing may be withheld from someone through poverty, or through the conditions of civilization into which he is born; but for the attainment of knowledge and proficiency in the higher worlds, there is no obstacle for those who earnestly seek them.

—RUDOLF STEINER

DAY 123

Meaning can only be understood in relation to its environment. Therefore, the words only make full sense in context. . . . There are no absolutes, there is no meaning without relationships, everything is not only interacting but interdependent. The kahunas use this idea to help give a person a powerfully secure sense of significance, while at the same time teaching him that to heal himself is to heal the world, and to heal the world is to heal himself. This is not a loss of individuality, but an understanding that individuality itself is a relationship with the environment.

—SERGE KING
Kahuna Healing

DAY 124

Mystical knowledge is power, and power will always tend to corrupt. Spiritual wisdom is the priceless key to those who earnestly desire to help others, as well as to attain personal joy and happiness—and is equally the dangerous master of those who wish to control others, who seek only personal benefit. When used with unselfish motive, there is no end to the wonders such knowledge can materialize. But if used for selfish purpose, it will inevitably boomerang back upon the user all manner of tragedies and disasters. This is one of the great laws of the Universe, which cannot be broken. It is inflexible, unswerving, and eternally undefeated.

—LINDA GOODMAN
Linda Goodman's Star Signs

DAY 125

Not once in a thousand times is it possible to achieve anything worth achieving except by labor, by effort, by serious purpose and by willingness to take risks.

—THEODORE ROOSEVELT

DAY 126

Materialistic success can be explained quite simply. Those who succeed focus their attention on success—not on their talent. Remember these words! All of their efforts are focused toward the upward movement rather than the perfection of their artistic ability. Neither do they allow anyone or anything to stand in the way of reaching their goals. This includes wives, families, friends and their children. They are prepared to pay the very high price that success demands.

—BRAD STEIGER
The World Beyond Death

DAY 127

Men are anxious to improve their circumstances, but are unwilling to improve themselves: they therefore remain bound.

—JAMES ALLEN
As You Think

DAY 128

There is only one way to get rid of faults and failings, and that is by clear recognition of them. Everything slumbers in the human soul and can be awakened. A person can even improve his intellect and reason if he makes it clear to himself why he is weak in this respect. Such self-knowledge is, of course, difficult, for the temptation to self-deception is immeasurably great. Anyone making a habit of being truthful to himself opens the portal leading to a deeper insight.

—RUDOLF STEINER

DAY 129

The ignorant work
for the fruit of their action:
The wise must work also
Without desire
Pointing man's feet
To the path of his duty.

—BHAGAVAD-GITA

DAY 130

You add suffering to the world just as much when you take offense as when you give offense.

—KEN KEYES, JR.
Handbook to Higher Consciousness

DAY 131

"You can get miles and miles of printout data," said Edgar Bronfman, Seagram's CEO. "You can buy packages and programs that will tell you in statistical terms everything you ever wanted to know about anything and maybe had the good sense not to ask. And while you're studying the passing parade of data, you may very well fail to hear the sound of opportunity knocking."

—ROY ROWAN
The Intuitive Manager

DAY 132

Faced with a decision and you can't find the answer? Try this: sit or stand straight to align your energy, and while looking out the window or at some point of concentration, fill your mind with white light. Then, to open you intuitive channels and allow your subconscious knowledge to provide you with the correct choice, place a piece of Lapis Lazuli or Azurite over your third eye. Listen to your inner voice, breathe deeply, and do not allow worry or confusion to intrude upon the light of illumination now filling your thoughts. Before long, you will have an answer.

—KEVIN SULLIVAN
The Crystal Handbook

DAY 133

The most beautiful experience we can have is the mysterious. It is the fundamental emotion which stands at the cradle of true art and true science. Whoever does not know it and can no longer wonder, no longer marvel, is as good as dead, and his eyes are dimmed.

—ALBERT EINSTEIN

DAY 134

In the warrior's path, women don't feel important
. . . because importance waters down fierceness.
In the warrior's path, women are fierce. They
don't demand anything, yet they are willing to
give anything of themselves. They fiercely seek a
signal from the spirit of things in the form of a
kind word, an appropriate gesture; and when they
get it, they express their thanks by redoubling
their fierceness.

In the warrior's path, women don't judge. They
fiercely reduce themselves to nothing in order to
listen, to watch, so they can conquer and be hum-
bled by their conquest or be defeated and enhanced by their defeat.

In the warrior's path, women don't surrender.
They may be defeated a thousand times, but they
never surrender. And above all, in the warrior's
path, women are free.

—FLORINDA DONNER
The Witch's Dream

DAY 135

In every created thing on earth there is an internal and an external; one of these is not given without the other, as there is no effect without a cause. . . . The external is estimated from the internal, and not the reverse.

—EMANUEL SWEDENBORG

DAY 136

Knowledge is the antidote to fear.

—EMERSON

DAY 137

Do not think of this, that or the other particular circumstances of health, peace, etc., but of health, peace, and prosperity themselves. . . . Think of the things rather than this or that condition of them. And then by the sure operation of the Universal Law these things will form themselves into the shapes best suited to your particular case, and will enter your life as active, living forces, which will never depart from you because you know them to be part and parcel of your own being.

—THOMAS TROWARD
The Hidden Power

DAY 138

There is no absurdity so palpable but that it may be firmly planted in the human head if only you begin to incubate it before the age of five by constantly repeating it with an air of great solemnity.

—SCHOPENHAUER

DAY 139

A man who's steadfast
in joy as in calamity
is one who has
achieved at last
God-given sanity.

—ANGELUS SILESIUS
The Book of Angelus Silesius

DAY 140

Intuitive flashes come day or night, even in the middle of a sound sleep. They come in a conference, on a hike, at the opera, during a party, down in a subway or up in a plane, but most often while you're concentrating on something else. Inventor Art Fry of 3M was singing in a choir and needed bookmarks that wouldn't fall out of his hymnal when he got the idea for Post-It notes, those ubiquitous peelable little yellow memos with a strip of stickum on the back. The crucial point is don't tune out your hunch. Don't let Monitor, the logical left hemisphere of your brain, talk you out of a sudden intuitive perception.

It's easy to intellectualize or analyze your way out of heeding a hunch. The trouble is you know, but you don't know how you know. So remind yourself that this fleeting feeling, this little whisper from deep inside your brain, may contain far more information—both facts and impressions—than you're likely to obtain from hours of analysis.

—ROY ROWAN
The Intuitive Manager

DAY 141

Dream lofty dreams, and as you dream, so shall you become. Your Vision is the promise of what you shall one day be; your ideal is the prophecy of what you shall at last unveil. The greatest achievement was at first and for a time a dream.

—JAMES ALLEN
As You Think

DAY 142

What you say is what you get.

—SHARON C. BROWN, PAT A. PAULSON, AND
JO ANN WOLF
Living on Purpose

DAY 143

The Pink Bubble

Exercise:

Sit or lie down comfortably, close your eyes and breathe deeply, slowly and naturally. Gradually relax deeper and deeper.

Imagine something that you would like to manifest. Imagine that it has already happened. Picture it as clearly as possible in your mind.

Now in your mind's eye surround your fantasy with a pink bubble; put goal inside the bubble. Pink is the color associated with the heart, and if this color vibration surrounds whatever you visualize, it will bring to you only that which is in perfect affinity with your being.

The third step is to let go of the bubble and imagine it floating off into the universe, still containing your vision. This symbolizes that you are emotionally "letting go" of it. Now it is free to float around in the universe, attracting and gathering energy for its manifestation.

There is nothing more you need to do.

—SHAKTI GAWAIN
Creative Visualization

DAY 144

The key to conscious listening is flexibility. Through listening, we have the ability to seek out and enter sound. When we freely resonate with sound(s) we enter into and become the sound. We are viewing the world through the sound and learn that sounds do not explain themselves. Sounds reveal themselves. There are as many revelations as there are sounds and combinations of sounds, but we have to be flexible and free to move through the various realities that sounds create.

—JOHN BEAULIEU
Music and Sound in the Healing Arts

DAY 145

Our thought as feeling is the magnet which draws
to us those conditions which accurately correspond
to itself. . . . Think from that interior standpoint
where there are no circumstances, and from whence
you can dictate what circumstances shall be, and
then leave the circumstances to take care of
themselves.

—THOMAS TROWARD
The Hidden Power

DAY 146

Remember that all is One, and look into yourself as you would understand your neighbor, your friend, your foe. For what you do to your neighbor, your friend or your foe, is a reflection of what you think of your Creator.

Hold fast to these truths, knowing that your life is an expression of the divine, that your health is an expression of your faith and hope in that divine power within your own self.

—EDGAR CAYCE

DAY 147

Accuse not nature. She hath done her part;
Do thou but thine.

—MILTON

DAY 148

Scientists with a lyrical turn of mind tell us that every form has its own characteristic "music," and that each object in the room is humming a different tune, outside the range of anyone's hearing, but humming just the same. It is said that cathedrals with their exquisite proportions are basically edifices of frozen music. Every object, every statue, every person has its own unique song to sing, depending on its shape and the materials of which it is made. Even you and I, if only we had the ears attuned to hear, are resonating with a strange music, trademarks of our own individual selves. The universe, it has been eloquently stated, is essentially a vast system of music.

—FRANCES WOSMEK
Acknowledge the Wonder

DAY 149

Imagination is a potent help in every event of our lives. Imagination acts on Faith, and both are the draughtsmen who prepare the sketches for Will to engage, more or less deeply, on the rocks of obstacles and oppositions with which the path of life is strewn.

—H. P. BLAVATSKY
Studies in Occultism

DAY 150

Imagination is the beginning of creation. You imagine what you desire; you will what you imagine, and at last you create what you will.

—GEORGE BERNARD SHAW

DAY 151

A poet may do more for a country than the owner of a nail factory.

—THEODORE ROOSEVELT

DAY 152

Your circumstances may be uncongenial, but they shall not long remain so if you but perceive an ideal and strive to reach it. You cannot travel *within* and stand still *without*.

—JAMES ALLEN
As You Think

DAY 153

When the will and the imagination are in conflict,
it is always the imagination that wins.

—EMILE COUE
*Self-Mastery through
Conscious Auto-suggestion*

DAY 154

No power alters the law of your own mind, but a power which knows the law of your mind can use it. Therefore, it is so essential that you should know the law of your own mind and realize its continual amenability to suggestion. That being so, the great thing is to get a standard for fundamental, unchangeable, and sufficient suggestion to which you can always turn, and which is automatically impressed upon your subconscious mind so deeply that no counter-suggestion can ever take its place; and that is the mystery of Christ, the Son of God.

—THOMAS TROWARD
The Hidden Power

DAY 155

A chief event of life is the day in which we have encountered a mind that startled us.

—EMERSON

DAY 156

A child finds himself by the constant weighing of himself in relationship to his guardians. He grows "through" the adults in whom he has come to have confidence and respect; and when he is ready to try his own weight, he pushes away. His readiness for life will depend upon the moment-to-moment worth of his relationships. If these have been trivial or unhealthy, he will never awaken, never become educated. If they have been wisely instrumental, intelligence will have found a place of operation, and he will have come into his own natural inheritance. In a word, he will be educated.

—VIRGINIA BURDEN TOWER
The Process of Intuition

DAY 157

The "Think Blue" Test

Once one has had a conscious experience of color as energy, it is not difficult to recall, reminisce, or meditate on a particular color, a series of colors, or innumerable combinations or blendings of colors.

Although this Test can be done anywhere, a quiet spot is very helpful. Before you begin, give yourself a few moments to relax and change the pace of your previous preoccupation.

1. Close your eyes and choose a color you would enjoy experiencing again.

2. Visualize the color you decide upon. Satisfy yourself that it is the shade you want: However, if this makes you anxious, simply accept whatever shade comes to mind.

3. Try to get a sense of the color you are visualizing. Ask yourself: What is it that I experience when I think "blue"?

4. Note your impressions just as they come to mind and allow your mind to associate ideas. If you find your mind wandering, gently bring it back to the question: What is it that I experience when I think "blue"?

5. When you have experienced the color blue to your satisfaction, go on to another color. If necessary, and if you wish, this Test can be extended over several days. However, most people will find that a concentration of five minutes, or at the most, ten minutes, is adequate for later recall. Do not allow yourself to become rigid in your expec-

Continued

tations. Experience all the dimensions of which you are capable when you ask yourself the question: What do I experience when I think "blue"?

—DOLORES KRIEGER
The Therapeutic Touch

DAY 158

Those who of old were good practicers of Tao did not use it to make the people bright, but rather used it to make them simple.

—LAO TZU

DAY 159

Mind, n. A mysterious form of matter secreted by the brain. Its chief activity consists in the endeavor to ascertain its own nature, the futility of the attempt being due to the fact that it has nothing but itself to know itself with.

—AMBROSE BIERCE

DAY 160

In essence, quartz crystals are tuning forks vibrating on multidimensional octaves of Light. Just as a tuning fork evokes a like-vibrational response from a receptive medium, so crystals facilitate an attunement with the harmonic vibrational tonalities of Light. These tools of Light resonate with the Light within each individual and thus assist in the process of evolutionary unfoldment. For this is their primary function—to evoke a like-response, a light response, in serving as interdimensional windows of Light.

It is crucially important to perceive and use crystals as tools—as very helpful, though not necessary, means of self-transformation. . . . The crystal is not a message unto itself; it acts only as a tool through which the inner Light of one's own being is clarified. It is always of the utmost importance to look first and foremost to the wisdom of inner guidance, the "still, small voice within." In this way the quartz crystal helps to evoke greater attunement with the "inner crystal" that is our very own Highter Self.

—RANDALL N. BAER AND VICKI V. BAER
Windows of Light

DAY 161

The whole of science is nothing more than a refinement of everyday thinking.

—ALBERT EINSTEIN

DAY 162

There is an overwhelming feeling of love that abides in that spiritual region. It becomes at once a part of your life essence. It is a type of love that is unconditional. This is the heavenly love of the Source. It is this love that we must try to emulate. When we love all living things unconditionally, we flow with God. It is then that we truly love God, for to love all that lives is to love the Source of all life. . . .

You should always enter meditation with the sole purpose of gaining awareness. You should first fill your entire being with unconditional love for all living things, beginning with your feet and continuing upward, including your head.

—BRAD STEIGER
The World Beyond Death

DAY 163

For the kahuna, belief is the fundamental basis for experience of any reality. The idea is that our experience is conditioned by what we believe, and we can only experience what we do believe is possible at some level of consciousness. The more firmly we believe something, the more profoundly it affects our experience.

—SERGE KING
Kahuna Healing

DAY 164

Relationship . . . is the mirror in which you discover yourself. Without relationship you are not; to be is to be related; to be related is existence. You exist only in relationship; otherwise you do not exist; existence has no meaning. It is not because you think you are that you come into existence. You exist because you are related; and it is the lack of understanding of relationship that causes conflict.

—KRISHNAMURTI

DAY 165

Patience has the effect of attraction, impatience the effect of repulsion on the treasures of higher knowledge. In the higher regions of existence, nothing can be attained by haste and unrest. Above all things, desire and craving must be silenced, for these are qualities of the soul before which all higher knowledge shyly withdraws.

—RUDOLF STEINER

DAY 166

Mind is the master power that molds and makes,
And we are Mind, and evermore we take
The tool of thought, and shaping what we will,
Bring forth a thousand joys, a thousand ills.
We think in secret, and it comes to pass—
Environment is but our looking glass.

—JAMES ALLEN
As You Think

DAY 167

Individualization is the key to power, and until we have resolutely determined to think our own thoughts and embody them in our own personalities, we shall show forth far more of the general expectancy of the period than any special state which answers our own determinate resolve. To regenerate a wasted organism may be a more difficult task than to prevent deterioration before it has set in.

—W. J. COLVILLE

DAY 168

It is not all of life to live, nor all of death to die;
for one is the birth of the other when viewed from
the whole or the center, and is but the experience
of an entity in its transitions to and from that
universal center from which all radiation takes
place.

—EDGAR CAYCE

DAY 169

Advice is like snow; the softer it falls the longer it dwells upon and the deeper it sinks into the mind.

—COLERIDGE

DAY 170

People are always blaming their circumstances for what they are. I don't believe in circumstances. The people who get on in this world are the people who get up and look for the circumstances they want, and if they can't find them, make them.

—GEORGE BERNARD SHAW

DAY 171

The whole thing about techniques is the idea that you need certain methods to make things work for you, when all you have to do is let things alone: Then they "work" for you automatically. If you forget that fact, then you'll always be looking for better and better methods . . . which will never really work . . . because Nature and your own nature work best when left alone.

If you're going to study such issues at all, then look for what you do right, and you'll always find that in those areas you let yourself alone and do what comes naturally, because you are inclined in that direction.

When you concentrate on what's wrong, you almost always try too hard, look for methods that will work better than the ones you're using now . . . when the truth is that the methods themselves stand in the way, whatever they are. Because Nature doesn't use methods. It "works" because it is what it is.

Methods presuppose the opposite in whatever area of your concern. They show your belief that nature doesn't work right on its own.

—JANE ROBERTS
The Further Education of Oversoul Seven

DAY 172

A monk asks:
—Is there anything more miraculous
than the wonders of nature?
The master answers:
—Yes, your awareness of the wonders of nature.

—ANGELUS SILESIUS
The Book of Angelus Silesius

DAY 173

Your dreams can become reality, so make sure you are thinking big enough.

—SHARON C. BROWN, PAT A. PAULSON, AND
JO ANN WOLF
Living on Purpose

DAY 174

The Hell to be endured hereafter, of which theology tells, is no worse than the hell we make for ourselves in this world by habitually fashioning our characters in the wrong way.

—WILLIAM JAMES

DAY 175

If you have once felt the functioning of a faculty in yourself beyond and above reason, you will probably be willing to "put your weight on it," until little by little, it finally becomes the very headquarters of your existence.

At first, in small ways, you will feel a hunch and notice it becomes borne out in due course, but as the process grows, you may very well learn that the test of reason does not apply and that you may need to wait a long time to see the wisdom of certain promptings that come to you. To the beginner, it is a most difficult phase when he oscillates between self-trust and distrust, wanting so much to return to the good, "safe" handholds at the edge of the wharf and leave the swimming to somebody else! Reason then seems a very comfortable raft to cling to—however limited in its reach—and ignorance has a cozy sound. Sooner or later, however, the urge to venture forth outweighs every fear and impulse to retreat.

—VIRGINIA BURDEN TOWER
The Process of Intuition

DAY 176

We see things not as they are—but as we are.

—KEN KEYES, JR.
Handbook to Higher Consciousness

DAY 177

Knowledge is the knowing that we cannot know.

—EMERSON

DAY 178

Crystals and gemstones can be placed around the home to channel energy constructively throughout your living quarters. Crystal clusters and formations can be used as decorative items on coffee tables, bathtubs (one at each corner of the tub), kitchen counters, home workplaces, and sleeping areas. Crystal prisms can be hung from windows to send rays of color throughout the room when the window is getting sunlight. Crystals are highly effective placed on windowsills where they can get daily exposure to the sun. You can balance out the energy of any room if Quartz crystals are placed around the room with points directed north and west.

Recommended gemstones for the home are Turquoise, which protects against environmental pollutants; all varieties of Coral (except Black); Jade for its soothing qualities; Amber for its protective nature; Rose Quartz for love, tenderness, gentleness, and its ability to create a warm environment in which you can feel loved. Fluorite (dispels psychic clutter) . . . Black Tourmaline (repels negative energy) . . . Malachite/Azurite to soothe, calm the spirit . . . Smoky Quartz because it increases creativity, fertility, and joy.

—KEVIN SULLIVAN
The Crystal Handbook

DAY 179

Do what you can with what you've got, where you are.

—THEODORE ROOSEVELT

DAY 180

A mind not aware of itself—ordinary consciousness—is like a passenger strapped into an airplane seat, wearing blinders, ignorant of the nature of transportation, the dimension of the craft, its range, the flight plan, and the proximity of other passengers.

The mind aware of itself is pilot. True, it is sensitive to flight rules, affected by weather, and dependent on navigation aids, but still vastly freer than the "passenger" mind.

Anything that draws us into a mindful, watchful state has the power to transform, and anyone of normal intelligence can undertake such a process. Mind, in fact, is its own transformative vehicle, inherently prepared to shift into new dimensions if only we let it. Conflict, contradictions, mixed feelings, all the elusive material that usually swirls around the edges of awareness can be reordered at higher and higher levels. Each new integration makes the next easier.

—MARILYN FERGUSON
The Aquarian Conspiracy

DAY 181

A Zen student asked his *roshi* the most important element of Zen.

The *roshi* replied, "Attention."

"Yes, thank you," the student replied. "But can you tell me the second most important element?"

And the *roshi* replied, "Attention."

—DAN MILLMAN
Way of the Peaceful Warrior

DAY 182

The true value of a human being is determined primarily by the measure and the sense in which he has attained liberation from the self.

—ALBERT EINSTEIN

DAY 183

The question is not how much of the Presence of God you can bring into your life, but how much of your life can you bring into the present. The Presence of God is everywhere. You have only consciously to embrace it with your attention.

Once you have learned to focus your attention in the present moment, you can begin to refer to your intuitive faculties for direction. These intuitive sources are your direct link with the totality of your being. Trust them. They will not fail you . . . they can be your invaluable pilot in the present moment.

—KEN CAREY
The Starseed Transmissions

DAY 184

All there is in your life is the eternal now moment—
and your experience of the moment is created by
the programming in your head.

—KEN KEYES, JR.
Handbook to Higher Consciousness

DAY 185

Attention makes the bridge between ourselves and that "somewhat" not ourselves, which we know as the world of things. A rich, thick Universe, charged like a bank holiday crowd with infinite and unguessed possibilities of sight, sound and smell waits at our door; and waits for the most part in vain. Attention keeps the turnstile, rejects the many and admits the few. The direction toward which the turnstile is set conditions the aspect of the world which we are to know; the pace at which it works ensures that a certain number of sense impressions shall be received by us, deliver their message, and set up responsive movements on our part.

So too with the life of spirit. Though lived upon higher levels, it is not further removed from action; only the form of its action, the nature of its correspondences is changed with that change of rhythm which makes us free of a wider universe. The object here is the transcending of the merely physical, the obtaining of a foothold in Eternity; and Attention, Perception, Response must still be the means by which she moves toward that end.

—EVELYN UNDERHILL
The Mystic Way

DAY 186

Apart from man, no being wonders at its own existence.

—SCHOPENHAUER

DAY 187

Music has no value or morals. Music does not think. When music replaces our thoughts we are in trance and are open to suggestion. There is no longer a question of thinking. We are in motion. We are merged as one with the music. Our thoughts, emotions, and physical bodies are moving with the elemental qualities of the sound. Later, the self remembers. Music is always a participatory and energetic event. The difference between what is secular and what is divine in music is only a matter of focus. The divine is always present.

—JOHN BEAULIEU
Music and Sound in the Healing Arts

DAY 188

If you wish to reach the stage of enjoying everything, then seek enjoyment in nothing.

—SAINT JOHN OF THE CROSS

DAY 189

Everything factual is, in a sense, theory. The blue of the sky exhibits the basic laws of chromatics. There is no sense in looking for something behind phenomena: they *are* theory.

—GOETHE

DAY 190

Everything is dual; everything has poles; everything has its pair of opposites; like and unlike are the same; opposites are identical in nature, but different in degree; extremes meet; all truths are but half-truths; all paradoxes may be reconciled.

—*The Kybalion*

DAY 191

Human strength is not in extremes but in avoiding extremes.

—EMERSON

DAY 192

The nature of the mind is like a highly polished mirror, whereas the individual thoughts, emotions, impulses, feelings, sensations, etc., which arise are like the reflections in this mirror. . . . With presence and awareness we live in the condition of the mirror, so to speak, whereas with ignorance we live in the condition of the reflections, thinking that whatever appears before us is substantial and real.

—NAMKHAI NORBU
The Cycle of Day and Night

DAY 193

Genius means little more than the faculty of perceiving in an unhabitual way.

—WILLIAM JAMES

DAY 194

Clairaudient powers, like every other power which
enables man to raise the operations of the subjec-
tive mind above the threshold of consciousness,
may to one who knows the laws which govern it,
who appreciates its powers, and who is aware of
its limitations, become a source of decided advan-
tage. But to one who does not understand those
laws, powers, and limitations, those faculties may
prove to be like the wand in the hand of the slave
of the magician in the Eastern tale. He saw his
master wave his wand, and heard him give orders
to the spirits who arose at his command. The
slave stole the wand, waved it in the air, and
summoned the spirits. They came at his summons, but tore him in pieces instead of obeying
his commands. He had not observed that his master used his left hand for the purpose of conjuration.

The fate of the magician's slave was no worse
than that which may befall any man who irregu-
larly summons his own spirit, without understanding the laws which enable him to control it and
make it useful instead of destructive. He is conjur-
ing with the most potent force of nature below
that of Omnipotence.

—THOMSON JAY HUDSON
The Law of Psychic Phenomena

DAY 195

Life must be lived as play.

—PLATO

DAY 196

When the consciousness is still, there comes to it the awareness of its true and original nature.

—PATANJALI
Yoga Sutras

DAY 197

Do your duty always, but without attachment.
That is how a man reaches the ultimate Truth; by
working without anxiety about results.

—BHAGAVAD-GITA

DAY 198

To bring about a state of renewed youth it is necessary to return to the view of life which was ours in youth—not indeed to go back to intellectual infancy, but to fulfill the spirit of the gospel words, "Except ye . . . become as little children, ye shall not enter into the kingdom of heaven." The singular beauty and impressiveness of the childlike nature consists in this: that it takes every day as it comes and makes the most of it, all the while looking forward to a higher state and confidently expecting its realization. Two other states of mind are absolutely necessary alike to the retention and restoration of youth; first, a quiet, contented spirit, so grounded in true optimism that it sees the good in every experience and gathers joy and satisfaction from every changing scene; and second, a confident, aspiring temperament which sees through the veil of the present a far more glorious future, and instead of complaining of immediate circumstances as if they were detrimental to progress, sees in every phase of environment a means of passing to a higher state.

—W. J. COLVILLE

DAY 199

Change is the nursery of music, joy, life, and eternity.

—DONNE

DAY 200

The ultimate purpose of our life is to rejoin God in conscious participation of divinity.

—EDGAR CAYCE

DAY 201

Nearly all spiritual practices are based on attention. In fact, whenever you think you have lost the path, or whenever you feel confused by esoteric terminology or technique, remember that all these techniques or teachings are various ways to help you learn to pay attention.

—RICK FIELDS
Chop Wood, Carry Water

DAY 202

Man's mind, stretched to a new idea, never goes back to its original dimension.

—OLIVER WENDELL HOLMES

DAY 203

Habits are the shorthand of behavior.

—JULIE HENDERSON
The Lover Within

DAY 204

If you want to get a clearer view of any subject than you have at present, address yourself mentally to the abstract soul of that subject, and ask it to tell you about itself, and you will find that it will do so. I do not say that it will do this in any miraculous manner, but what you already know of the subject will range itself into a clearer order, and you will see connections that have not previously occurred to you. Then again, you will find that information of the class required will begin to flow towards you through quite ordinary channels, books, newspapers or conversation, without your especially laying yourself out to hunt for it; and again, at other times, ideas will come into your mind, you do not know how, but illuminating the subject with a fresh light.

—THOMAS TROWARD
The Law and the Word

DAY 205

Concentration is the secret of strength in politics, in war, in trade, in short in all the management of human affairs.

—EMERSON

DAY 206

It takes years for average persons in the nagual's world to remove themselves from their involvement with themselves and be capable of seeing the wonder of it all.

—FLORINDA DONNER
The Witch's Dream

DAY 207

There is no safe way to live. Living itself brings risk and growth. When you live on the edge choosing what is, you are living with awareness about yourself.

—SHARON C. BROWN, PAT A. PAULSON, AND JO ANN WOLF
Living on Purpose

DAY 208

To reason only whether a thing is so or not is like reasoning about the fit of a cap or a shoe without ever putting it on.

—EMANUEL SWEDENBORG

DAY 209

Nature magically suits the man to his fortunes by making these the fruit of his character.

—EMERSON

DAY 210

Love is built on love, which is in the totality of evolution and the totality of each one of us.

Let us drink profoundly of the communion of universal life.

Each day let us remind ourself that I AM.

—ALEX TANNOUS

DAY 211

The importance of the concept of "bodymind," that there is no separation between the body and the mind, cannot be stressed enough. We tend to think that we "have" a body, that we give our body exercise, food, rest, pleasure or medicine when "it" is ill. We see our body as something we carry around with us; we like parts of it but dislike other parts; we worry when something in it goes wrong, but what we usually fail to see is that it is not a part going wrong, it is the whole of ourself. When we feel depressed, our body feels heavy and lifeless; when we feel happy, we feel light and vibrant. Our mind and body work as one.

—GASTON ST. PIERRE AND DEBBIE BOATER
The Metamorphic Technique

DAY 212

Mental remedies are dependent for success upon mental conditions, just as physical remedies are dependent for their efficacy upon physical conditions.

—THOMSON JAY HUDSON
The Law of Mental Medicine

DAY 213

The body is the servant of the mind.
It obeys the operations of the mind,
whether they be deliberately chosen
or automatically expressed.

—JAMES ALLEN
As You Think

DAY 214

The physical universe was created when Oneness became duality, and we can see this duality, this yin and yang, everywhere in the universe, in every atom, every action, and in every function of the human body. Yin and yang are manifest everywhere, except at the very center of being, the perfect point of balance, at that infinite moment when the future becomes the past.

In the very center of a flower, a seed, or leaf bud, there is a point from which the energy is coming and from which growth proceeds. From that point the seed grows, the flower bud blooms. If you cut an apple or a cabbage in half you can see that it radiates from a central point. If you carefully examine the flower bud, leaf bud, seed, fruit, or vegetable, and dissect them until you come to their very center, you will find . . . nothing. Really there is only one thing, one energy, one consciousness, but in order to manifest itself it becomes yin and yang. In striving for health and harmony, we try to find that point of balance between yin and yang.

—ROBERT B. TISSERAND
The Art of Aromatherapy

DAY 215

The witch doctor succeeds for the same reason all the rest of us succeed. Each patient carries his own doctor inside him. They come to us not knowing that truth. We are best when we give the doctor who resides within each patient a chance to go to work.

—ALBERT SCHWEITZER

DAY 216

Cheerfulness is health; the opposite, melancholy, is disease.

—SHAKESPEARE

DAY 217

Anyone who wishes to help "make better" must develop a deep sense of love and compassion, which is a reflection of one's spiritual self in union with nature and Source. One must be willing to explore his own illnesses and loneliness and welcome change. Through the looking within, we may become truly empty, leaving space to be filled by That which is Above. We attach to and personalize our illnesses, claiming them as our own—my migraine, my cancer, my broken life. It seems the two-legged has a propensity for suffering. We cling to our psychosis and disease. If we give over our pain, what then will take its place?

We must practice surrender in our every moment, in our everyday lives. If we develop the quality of balance and emptiness, we will be working in harmony with the forces of nature and spirit all the time, therefore having a stronger effect for good in the world.

—OH SHINNAH
in *Five Great Healers Speak Here*

DAY 218

Nature never deceives us; it is always we who deceive ourselves.

—ROUSSEAU

DAY 219

We should treat our minds as innocent and ingenuous children whose guardians we are—be careful what objects and what subjects we thrust on their attention.

—THOREAU

DAY 220

The wrong belief which externalizes as sickness is the belief that some secondary cause, which is really only a condition, is a primary cause.

—THOMAS TROWARD
The Edinburgh Lectures on Mental Science

DAY 221

If you're the type of person who is concerned with having a beautiful physical image, but who has little patience and some difficulty with self-discipline in following a diet, you may need some strong energy to help. Begin by putting away all your favorite "flashy" gemstones. Try some new energy-support stones. Select an earth agate or a jasper, a garnet or a malachite, or even a bloodstone. They will secure your strength as you are beautifying yourself. They'll not overstimulate your desire for food, but will aid your energy while you're disciplining yourself. Avoid your expensive diamonds and sapphires. Remove your chrysocolla and cover up your crystals. Be not only secure with your diet plan, but mentally relaxed and calm while you're obtaining your fantastic new image. Shine later when you are lighter. . . .

Jaspers and agates are most often considered the all-around good diet stones. Jaspers can aid you physically by their color: red, orange, brown and green; and by their compact, dense energy. Agates can help you feel secure, as they are the natural earth stones.

—DOROTHEE L. MELLA
Stone Power

DAY 222

When most people say "scientist," they mean "technician." A technician is a highly trained person whose job is to apply known techniques and principles. He deals with the known. A scientist is a person who seeks to know the true nature of physical reality. He deals with the unknown.

In short, scientists discover and technicians apply. However, it is no longer evident whether scientists really discover new things or whether they *create* them. Many people believe that "discovery" is actually an act of creation. If this is so, then the distinction between scientists, poets, painters and writers is not clear. In fact, it is possible that scientists, poets, painters and writers are all members of the same family of people whose gift it is by nature to take those things which we call commonplace and to *re-present* them to us in such ways that our self-imposed limitations are expanded. Those people in whom this gift is especially pronounced, we call geniuses.

—GARY ZUKAV
The Dancing Wu Li Masters

DAY 223

To feel young one must continually feed upon new thought. The body needs constant supplies of fresh air and nutriment, and the mind has its needs that are no less exacting.

—W. J. COLVILLE

DAY 224

Who never wins can rarely lose,
Who never climbs as rarely falls

—WHITTIER

DAY 225

Your body, together with the spirit that inhabits it is like a sitar. If you do not understand the instrument, you cannot create music. You have learned your way around the world, but you are still a mystery to yourself. If it were not so, you could perform miracles, for the human mind has an infinite resource which you have so far only encountered in vivid glimpses, short as heat lightning but held fast in the memory forever, for they were the reality of your life's experience.

All any teacher can do is show you the path. You have to walk it alone.

—GURUDEV SHREE CHITRABHANU
in *Five Great Healers Speak Here*

DAY 226

Think health and talk health on all suitable occasions, remembering that under the law of suggestion health may be made contagious as well as disease.

—THOMSON JAY HUDSON
The Law of Mental Medicine

DAY 227

Yet there is a need for us to lift up our physical eyes and hands to the starry heaven above. I mean when and if the spirit moves, not otherwise. For the things of the body are subject to those of the spirit and are controlled thereby, not the other way round.

—THE CLOUD OF UNKNOWING

DAY 228

The people who live in fear of disease are the people who get it. Anxiety quickly demoralizes the whole body and lays it open to the entrance of disease.

—JAMES ALLEN
As You Think

DAY 229

It is the last lesson of modern science, that the highest simplicity of structure is produced not by few elements, but by the highest complexity.

—EMERSON

DAY 230

Know that no urge—astrologically, numerologically, symbolically—surpasses the will of the entity in any experience. For there is that within self that is creative; and it, that creative force, cooperating with the divine without, will lead to the choice of that which is life. And when the choice is made, then there may be a vision, astrologically and otherwise, of what the end thereof is. But each soul is given the birthright of the ability to choose—under any environment, any circumstance, any experience!

—EDGAR CAYCE

DAY 231

The five colors can blind,
The five tones deafen,
The five tastes cloy.
The race, the hunt, can drive men mad
And their booty leave them no peace.
Therefore a sensible man
Prefers the inner to the outer eye:
He has his yes,—he has his no.

—LAO TZU

DAY 232

Your emotions create disturbance and imbalance, because they are so changeable. It is giving a lot of control to someone else if you have decided that their morning call or their particular mood can emotionally influence your day. You can end up living your day experiencing their emotion.

Feelings, on the other hand, can add color to your life and tell you a lot about yourself. You can separate feelings from emotions by recognizing the genesis of them. The genesis of feelings is you, and the genesis of emotions is something or someone else. Feelings have an energy that originates internally that may or may not have to do with an external experience.

You experience loving from the inside and then you notice that love on the outside finds you.

—SHARON C. BROWN, PAT A. PAULSON, AND
JO ANN WOLF
Living on Purpose

DAY 233

You need to know the great power that lies
in the act of visualization.

Vision is spiritual reality, and all things
that exist in your world first existed in spirit.
The concept comes first, the physical,
which is denser matter, follows.

Once you challenge your preconceptions,
they become misconception.
The diameters of your awareness expand.
A wall, for instance, is no longer only a wall
but a bit of moving, vibrating consciousness.

Anything that can be envisioned
can be brought into your physical reality.

—EMMANUEL

DAY 234
Toning

We express ourselves with words and sounds. Beneath these words are the vibrations of the tone upon which they travel. Tone is an underlying force operating in our lives. It is the voice not only of our thoughts, but primarily of our physical body.

To do toning, stand comfortably erect and let your body sway as a flower on its stalk in a breeze. Relax your jaw so that your teeth are slightly parted.

Let sound come up from your feet, not down from your mind. Begin with an audible groan, such as "ohhhh" or "ahhhhh" and let it give you a feeling of release, of emptying out, of resting.

Let your body groan as long as it likes, until the tones your body makes surface spontaneously.

Let the toning session last ten minutes or an hour—until your body feels cleansed and nourished and a sigh is released. The sigh lets you know that the body-voice is satisfied.

It is hard to describe scientifically what happens during the toning. When you do it, you know that you feel good, as though something important inside you has been accomplished. Perhaps it is that the whole person has been brought into harmony once again.

—STEVEN HALPERN AND LOUIS SAVERY
Sound Health

DAY 235

Music is a force beyond our thought, our culture and our history. It transcends our associations. All music is potentially healing.

—JOHN BEAULIEU.

DAY 236

The physically weak man can make himself strong by careful and patient training, so the man of weak thoughts can make them strong by exercising himself in right thinking.

—JAMES ALLEN
As You Think

DAY 237

Happiness is the best antidote for disease.

—C. F. BATES
in *The Metaphysical Magazine*, 1895

DAY 238

All mental wounding, from sexual abuse to racial harassment, results in distrust. That is why it is of such prime importance that therapists who wish to serve those with such deep mental bonding clear themselves of "healers' disease," the need for someone else to be different as a means of bargaining with their own sense of helplessness and unworthiness. It is by understanding the intention behind our touch that we break the knee-jerk emergency reaction to suffering. It defines the importance of the work on ourselves, which allows us to touch with love that which has been fearfully rejected. It is another example of how working on ourselves is of benefit to all so that we do not touch with need but instead offer love.

—STEPHEN LEVINE
Healing into Life and Death

DAY 239

To take old duties in a new way; to rename seeming obstacles and call them all privileges and opportunities; to resolve to find the good of which we are in search through the medium of common occurrences; in a word, to take an altered stand with reference to all people and things about us, and that stand a bright and hopeful one, is to drive away the furrows of care which have already creased our cheeks; to keep away the coming wrinkles; and best of all, to prevent the embittering of life which is the secret spring whence all decrepitude proceeds.

—W. J. COLVILLE

DAY 240

The healing of our relationship with place begins
with the preservation of the natural environment.
We cannot go to the wild for renewal if no wilderness is left.

—STARHAWK
Truth or Dare

DAY 241

A man is about as happy as he makes up his mind to be.

—ABRAHAM LINCOLN

DAY 242

Colors are the deeds and sufferings of Light.

—GOETHE

DAY 243

Healing often begins with our bodies, but it does not end there. If we view ourselves as the universe in microcosm, then our lives become a laboratory for testing the power of healing attitudes. When we find that meditation and prayer, for example, bring peace and health to our bodies, then by expanding our awareness, we can begin to trust that these same healing attitudes and practices can bring healing to families, societies, and the planet as a whole. In this sense, healing becomes a way of being in the world—one in which we are living to bring greater flow and harmony to all.

—RICK FIELDS
Chop Wood, Carry Water

DAY 244

The right way is the natural way and the right instrument the natural instrument.

—PLATO

DAY 245

Rainbow Meditation

Sit in a comfortable chair, spine straight, holding a crystal in your left hand. Imagine at your feet a bright, glowing ball of violet color. See it as the pulsating, vibrant, violet energy of high spirituality, representing one who is searching for the deeper meanings of life and existence.

Let this ball expand and rise until it fills and permeates every atom of your body, drawing the Light energy upward until it comes out through the top of your head. Then see it explode with a flashing cascade of violet fire and flow down over you like an energizing fountain.

Repeat the procedure with the rich, deep tones of indigo, for these colors represent the searcher who truly seeks his or her own purpose in Life.

Follow this with the same procedure using other colors: blue, which brings the feeling of Divine Guidance; green, reflecting great joy, anticipation and healing; yellow, representing deep thought or intellectual activity; orange, representing wisdom, justice, creativity and good will to all; and bright, clear, scintillating red which stands for vital, optimistic zest for life.

Try to visualize clear, bright colors but let your mind be free to bring in whatever associations it wishes as you draw each ball of color up through your body to explode in a shimmering cascade of color and energy down over your whole Being.

Do this exercise for three days. Then reverse

Continued

the procedure, going from red to violet. The first exercise will seem to draw your attention down and in; the second will draw your attention upward towards higher spiritual attunement.

—KORRA DEAVER
Rock Crystal, The Magic Stone

DAY 246

Nature makes nothing in vain.

—EMERSON

DAY 247

Love everyone unconditionally . . . including yourself.

—KEN KEYES, JR.
Handbook to Higher Consciousness

DAY 248

Strong, calm people are always loved and revered. They are like shade-giving trees in a thirsty land, or a sheltering rock in a storm.

—JAMES ALLEN
As You Think

DAY 249

When I am, as it were, completely myself, entirely alone, and of good cheer—say, traveling in a carriage, or walking after a good meal, or during the night when I cannot sleep; it is on such occasions that ideas flow best and most abundantly. Whence and how they come, I know not; nor can I force them.

—MOZART

DAY 250

The purpose of meditation, paradoxically, is to learn to be without purpose. Since nearly everything we do in life is done with some goal in mind, most of our actions are only means to an end, pointing us continually toward a future that does not exist. But meditation, when no goal disturbs it, allows us to discover the richness and profundity of the present moment. We begin to realize the miraculous power of our own lives—not as they will be, or as we might imagine they once were at some golden time in the past, but as they actually are. Meditation is one of the few things in life that is not about DOING but about BEING.

—RICK FIELDS
Chop Wood, Carry Water

DAY 251

Never seek to leave your body if you desire to concentrate. On the contrary, make yourself as much at home as possible where you are; then LOOK out, but do not GO out.

—W. J. COLVILLE

DAY 252

Heard melodies are sweet, but those unheard are sweeter.

—KEATS

DAY 253

There is no need to run outside
For better seeing,
Nor to peer from a window. Rather abide
At the center of your being;
For the more you leave it, the less you learn.
Search your heart and see
If he is wise who takes each turn;
The way to do is to be.

—LAO TZU

DAY 254

How, then, to invite the lover within? If you experience yourself as the vessel that life penetrates, which is so, then all you have to do is to let that penetration touch you as fully and deeply as possible in every moment. . . .

For me, the way in has been to approach any place where I am withholding energy—keeping it in stasis—whether in my unexpressed longing for union, or my fear that I won't have enough money, or my anger at the man who didn't love me as I wanted him to. wherever there is energy in stasis, there is an engorgement, a honey pot waiting to flow, I do whatever I know how to allow the energy into my awareness, to encourage it to move, and then to surrender to it. . . . To the extent that we limit our possibilities for pleasure and orgasm to genital sexuality, we don't even consider these other possibilities—or they sound abstract or far off. For me, nothing is so exciting as to imagine that *life* is my lover—and is *always* courting me. To relate to life in that way is a challenge and a surrender that invites me deeper into being alive in every moment that I can manage it. . . . When I can trust opening past the possibility of having X to the possibility of satisfaction with or without it, then my capacity for pleasure expands.

—JULIE HENDERSON
The Lover Within

DAY 255

Nature is not governed except by obeying her.

—BACON

DAY 256

The keenest enjoyment of the wilderness is reserved for him who enjoys also the garnered wisdom of the present and the past.

—THEODORE ROOSEVELT

DAY 257

The secret of enjoying life is to take an interest in it.

—THOMAS TROWARD
The Law and the Word

DAY 258

The abstinent run away from what they desire
But carry their desires with them;
When a man enters Reality,
He leaves his desires behind him.

Even a mind that knows the path
Can be dragged from the path;
The senses are so unruly.
But he controls the senses
And recollects the mind
And fixes it on me.

I call him illumined.

—BHAGAVAD-GITA

DAY 259

It is the hardest thing to have complete experiences. We can't ever erase an old way of seeing things. We incorporate our dreams and live. Some of us are aware of it. We spin our psychic compass, our lives plunge into a terrain of feeling, desire, motives, the other and death. It brings us joy and sadness. Change has an erratic pace. The cast is broken before a mold is produced. We juggle the truth of life and find illumination every time we bump into our own worlds, completing experiences with the master. The true meaning of our past is preserved until we find it by going back. Beauty roars in stillness. It is tattooed in every human heart.

—CRAIG GRIFFETHS
Bright Cotton

DAY 260

Learning to trust one's intuition is something like learning to swim. The curious and mysterious fact is that we are all immersed in an invisible medium to which the intuitive person relates as the swimmer relates to water. In this medium, as in the ocean, there are currents, attractions, repulsions, vortices, proper rules of displacement and many other familiar properties, although the fact may be as hidden from the knowledge of the casual observer as the properties of water are hidden from the understanding of the landlubber. The key of access to this hidden knowledge consists of at least a spark of credulity (the spark itself cannot be there unless it arises from an intuitive source), a willingness to set aside beliefs and prejudices, and the will to face one's fear squarely. In this latter instance, the desire to overcome fear must actually be stronger than the desire to live. Impossible? There are those who have discovered that fear is death in life, and have willingly risked physical death and loss of all that is considered valuable in order to live in freedom.

—VIRGINIA BURDEN TOWER
The Process of Intuition

DAY 261

All existence is coexistence.

—HEIDEGGER

DAY 262

We're not different from anything else on Earth.
We're not separate from the tides that are pulled
back and forth by the moon. The water in our
bodies moves with the tides. We are a part of it
all. If we go to a place that has a vortex, we can
feel the energy. We can use it to trigger the recognition and the experience of infinity, to get out of
our finite minds. We can experience an energy
that can nourish us, that can expand us into our
multidimensional selves.

When we go someplace, on a vacation, we should
look for places that have vortices. Our emotional
bodies will let go when we enter into a frequency
that's higher than our own.

—CHRIS GRISCOM
Ecstasy Is a New Frequency

DAY 263

Often the message of illness is to be quieter and to spend some time just being in contact with our inner self. Illness often forces us to relax, let go of all our busyness and "efforting" and drop into a deep, quiet level of consciousness where we can receive the nourishing energy that we need.

The healing always comes from within. When we allow ourselves quiet and inner contact regularly, we no longer need to get sick in order for our inner self to get our attention.

—SHAKTI GAWAIN
Creative Visualization

DAY 264

A man is rich in proportion to the number of things which he can afford to let alone.

—THOREAU

DAY 265

This meditation exercise incorporates gemstones by color gradation. You can add or subtract gemstones as you feel the need; the ones recommended are not necessarily the only ones that can or should be used. . . .

Place a Smoky Quartz on your pelvic bone; Bloodstone, Garnet, or Ruby on your abdomen; Citrine or Topaz on your navel; Peridot or Green Tourmaline on your solar plexus; Rose Quartz or Rhodochrosite on your heart; Turquoise or Chrysocolla at your throat; Amethyst or Azurite in the middle of your forehead; and a Clear Quartz crystal at the crown of your head. Place a clear Quartz crystal in each palm and instep of each foot.

Lie quietly on the floor for fifteen to thirty minutes, relaxing and breathing deeply from your abdomen. When you are finished, remove the stones slowly and concentrate on what impressions you received.

—KEVIN SULLIVAN
The Crystal Handbook

DAY 266

If your consciousness can flow from one here-and-now experience to the next here-and-now experience, you are peacefully and beautifully flowing in the river of your life.

—KEN KEYES, JR.
Handbook to Higher Consciousness

DAY 267

Everything which is of strife makes the vision of the truth more difficult; everything which tends to controversy makes the grasping of the truth harder. The spirit of man should be like a lake unruffled by wind or storm. Under such conditions a lake will reflect perfectly the mountains which are around it and the sky above it. With an unruffled surface it will give a perfect reflection of these. If the wind sweeps over it or the storm ruffles it, its reflections are disturbed; they are not clear. The images will be seen, but not clearly. And so it is with the division of light and the human spirit. If the spirit is ruffled, then the Divine Image cannot mirror itself thereon. By love and not by hatred the spirit must grow. By a willingness to learn and not by dogmatism the love of the spirit is increased. The roads are many but the goal is one, and that is realized by every soul that really seeks for the Divine.

—ANNIE BESANT
in *The Metaphysical Magazine*, 1895

DAY 268

If right thought is kept well in the mind, no evil thing can ever enter there.

—BUDDHA

DAY 269

He who is always without passions beholds the mystery; he who always has passions beholds [only] the issues.

—LAO TZU

DAY 270

Like the Maya who preceded us, we shall understand that the path to the stars is through the senses and that proper utilization of our mind as the auto-regulatory control factor will help facilitate the passage to different levels or dimensions of being.

—JOSE ARGUELLES
The Mayan Factor

DAY 271

Sincere seekers for a meaningful ground to stand on in today's jungle of alternatives must be prepared to carry their own luggage. They will need a good supply of common sense, a little healthy skepticism, and the ability to stand their ground if the way of others does not seem to be their way. It is not important whether seekers choose to do their exploring and discovering inside a place of worship or outside one, their learning inside or outside the walls of academia. Some naturally prefer the greater flexibility of a "loner." Others need the support of a group. Just as each of us is unique, so should be the path of our connectedness.

—FRANCES WOSMEK
Acknowledge the Wonder

DAY 272

Fact can never be explained, since only another fact could explain it; therefore the existence of a universe rather than no universe, or of one sort of universe rather than another, must be accepted without demur.

—SANTAYANA

DAY 273

To know ourselves means to know our relationship with the world—not only the world of ideas and people, but with nature, with the things we possess. That is, our life—life being relationship to the whole.

—KRISHNAMURTI

DAY 274

One who recognizes all men as members of his own body is a sound man to guard them.

—LAO TZU

DAY 275

The evolution of quartz crystals is much different than ours in many ways, and very similar in others. Quartz crystals are conceived within the womb of the earth and matured there until they are born onto the surface of the planet, much in the same way that humans incubate within the warmth of the maternal womb while grounding their spirit into a physical body before entering the material world. Each crystal is unique and unlike any others, each with its own personality, lessons and experiences (as with humans). The purpose and destiny of both is to unite with cosmic consciousness and manifest that on the material plane. Crystals and humans can become working partners in that process and serve each other's evolution. When the mineral kingdom and the human kingdom link their forces together, new worlds of consciousness unfold. As the healing essence of quartz crystals vibrates the soul of humanity, vast horizons of hope and joy appear.

—KATRINA RAPHAELL
Crystal Enlightenment

DAY 276

We are such stuff
As dreams are made on, and our little life
Is rounded with a sleep.

—SHAKESPEARE

DAY 277

Nature gives up her innermost secrets and imparts true wisdom only to him who seeks truth for its own sake, and who craves for knowledge in order to confer benefits on others, not on his own unimportant personality. And as it is precisely to the personal benefit that nearly every candidate for adeptship and magic looks, and that few are they who consent to learn at such a heavy price and so small a benefit for themselves in prospect—the really wise Occultists become with every century fewer and rarer. How many are there, indeed, who would not prefer the will-o'-the-wisp of even passing fame to the steady and ever-growing light of eternal divine knowledge, if the latter has to remain, for all but oneself—a light under the bushel?

—H. P. BLAVATSKY
Studies in Occultism

DAY 278

As long as our civilization is essentially one of property, of fences, of exclusiveness, it will be mocked by delusions. Our riches will leave us sick; there will be bitterness in our laughter; and our wine will burn our mouth. Only that good profits which we can taste with all doors open, and which serves all men.

—EMERSON

DAY 279

Even when we get what we addictively want, our wanting to keep things that way automatically creates a new addiction.

—KEN KEYES, JR.
Handbook to Higher Consciousness

DAY 280

In the long run you hit only what you aim at.
Therefore, though you should fail immediately,
you had better aim at something high.

—THOREAU

DAY 281

There is no security in life, only opportunity.

—MARK TWAIN

DAY 282

Science is the branch of mysticism that deals with the measurable. Mysticism is the branch of science that deals with the unmeasurable.

—RA BONEWITZ
The Cosmic Crystal Spiral

DAY 283

The spiritual life is not a special career involving abstraction from the world of things. It is a part of every man's life, and until he has realized it he is not a complete human being, has not entered into possession of all his powers. It is therefore the function of a practical mysticism to increase, not diminish, the total efficiency, the wisdom and steadfastness of those who try to practise it.

—EVELYN UNDERHILL
Practical Mysticism

DAY 284

The use of affirmations, meditation and prayer, the study of the Scriptures, the practice of the virtues and the rendering of service to one's fellow man are methods often recommended by the readings for the attainment of a changed consciousness. But genuine growth cannot be mechanically induced. Unless and until the heart is sufficiently tenderized, these practices will be, in Paul's apt phrase, as tinkling brass; without true charity they are essentially worthless. As disciplines they will be valuable; as suggestive forces they will have an effect; as educative experiences they will start the soul on the proper path. But for those multitudes of souls who are at the kindergarten stage, spiritually speaking, they cannot lead immediately to college. Not all people are sufficiently evolved spiritually to be capable of achieving in one lifetime that all-consuming, all-embracing love which is the essence of the true Christ-consciousness, and thus achieve liberation from the debt of karma.

—EDGAR CAYCE

DAY 285

Keep your hand firmly upon the helm of thought.
In the bark of your soul reclines the commanding
Master; He does but sleep; wake Him. Self-control
is strength; Right Thought is mastery; Calmness
is power.

—JAMES ALLEN
As You Think

DAY 286

The whole natural world corresponds to the spiritual world: not only the natural world in general, but also every particular part thereof (i.e., in detail). The world of nature comes forth and subsists from the spiritual world, just as an effect does from its efficient cause.

—EMANUEL SWEDENBORG

DAY 287

The more we know of the fixed laws of nature, the more incredible do miracles become.

—CHARLES DARWIN

DAY 288

He who sees the inaction that is in action, and the action that is in inaction, is wise indeed. Even when he is engaged in action he remains poised in the tranquility of the Atman.

—BHAGAVAD-GITA

DAY 289

Unless you find paradise
At your own center
There is not the smallest chance
That you may enter.

—ANGELUS SILESIUS
The Book of Angelus Silesius

DAY 290

When you are the same on the inside as what people see on the outside, you are in touch with your own personal power.

Letting the world see you is letting the world know what you truly believe about your life.

What is some challenge that you could accept that would make you more visible?

Where are you hesitant about getting more visible?

How would your life change if you got more visible?

How much of your life is passing you by because you remain low-key?

—SHARON C. BROWN, PAT A. PAULSON, AND JO ANN WOLF
Living on Purpose

DAY 291

There is no place among us for the mere pessimist; no man who looks at life with a vision that sees all things black or gray can do aught healthful in molding the destiny of a mighty and vigorous people. But there is just as little use for the foolish optimist who refuses to face the many and real evils that exist, and who fails to see that the only way to insure the triumph of righteousness in the future is to war against all that is base, weak, and unlovely in the present.

—THEODORE ROOSEVELT

DAY 292

When we see men of worth, we should think of equaling them; when we see men of a contrary character, we should turn inward and examine ourselves.

—CONFUCIUS

DAY 293

Healing, like grace, can be somewhat disorienting in its early stages. It is a breaking through of the old to reveal the ever new. Healing, like grace, always takes us toward our true nature. Indeed, healing is not somewhere we are going, but a discovery of where we already are—a participation in the process unfolding moment to moment. Many of us pray for a miracle when all else has failed. We wish for grace to descend upon us. But grace comes from within. Grace arises when the work of healing is in process. A graceful healing into the spirit that goes beyond the need of definition or even words like "grace" or "karma" or "spirit." Though many of the people we worked with did not begin with a spiritual inclination, many uncovered their healing by taking on what some call spiritual practices toward the discovery of a deeper self. But we did notice that even those who had shied away from what they called "spiritual stuff" in the course of their daily confrontation with the impermanence of the body, cultivated a certain quality of heartfulness and peacefulness.

—STEPHEN LEVINE
Healing into Life and Death

DAY 294

The fundamental understanding of oneself does not come through knowledge or through the accumulation of experiences, which is merely the cultivation of memory. The understanding of oneself is from moment to moment; if we merely accumulate knowledge of the self, that very knowledge prevents further understanding, because accumulated knowledge and experience becomes the center through which thought focuses and has its being. The world is not different from us and our activities because it is what we are which creates the problems of the world: the difficulty with the majority of us is that we do not know ourselves directly but seek a system, a method, a means of operation by which to solve the many human problems.

—KRISHNAMURTI

DAY 295

The best soldier does not attack. The superior fighter succeeds without violence. The greatest conqueror wins without a struggle. . . . This is called intelligent nonaggressiveness. This is called mastery of men.

—LAO TZU

DAY 296

The greatest obstacle to being heroic is the doubt whether one may not be going to prove one's self a fool. The truest heroism is to resist the doubt; and the profoundest wisdom to know when it ought to be resisted, and when to be obeyed.

—HAWTHORNE

DAY 297

Love is the work of each one of us. It has no value unless it is made visible. Through love, the impossible is made possible for all generations to come.

When we see our work become a reality in the world for the world, this is the act of love.

—ALEX TANNOUS
Reflexions sur la Vie Interieure

DAY 298

The law of levity is as real as the law of gravity and has everything to do with release from attachment to self-importance. For in the end, the joke is on those that cannot rise above themselves to dally in the vast luminosity which the narrow chinks of selfhood withhold from entering the sense-body's neural cavern.

—JOSE ARGUELLES
The Mayan Factor

DAY 299

A generation goes, and a generation comes,
but the earth remains forever.
The sun rises and the sun goes down
and hastens to the place where it rises.
The wind blows to the south,
and goes around to the north;
around and around goes the wind,
and on its circuits it returns.
All streams run to the sea,
but the sea is not full. . . .
What has been is what will be,
and what has been done is what will be done;
there is nothing new under the sun.
Is there a thing of which it is said,
"See, this is new?"
It has already been
in the ages before us.

—Ecclesiastes 1:4–7a, 9–10

DAY 300

All rising to a great place is by a winding stair.

—BACON

DAY 301

Here . . . is an important rule for the student: know how to observe silence concerning your spiritual experiences. Yes, observe silence even toward yourself. Do not attempt to clothe in words what you contemplate in the spirit, or to pore over it with clumsy intellect. Lend yourself freely and without reservation to these spiritual impressions, and do not disturb them by reflecting or pondering over them too much. For you must remember that your reasoning faculties are by no means equal to your new experience. You have acquired these faculties in a life hereto confined to the physical world of the senses; the faculties you are now acquiring transcend this world. Do not try, therefore, to apply to the new and higher perceptions the standard of the old. Only he who has gained some certainty and steadiness in the observation of inner experiences can speak about them and thereby stimulate his fellow-men.

—RUDOLF STEINER

DAY 302

More than likely, we will never achieve the satisfaction of knowing a single "why" of our becoming, any more than our limited, earthbound brain could ever meaningfully grasp a clear purpose behind the vastness of the universe. Any answer would necessarily include understanding the why of the why, and that would be a little like looking into one's own eyes.

—FRANCES WOSMEK
Acknowledge the Wonder

DAY 303

The gods and the universe really begin everyplace and everywhere at once, at every point. Our psychological reality rises from an inner, inconceivable divine mind that's invisible to us, since we are It earthized, individualized. We're the gods in camouflage.

—JANE ROBERTS
The Further Education of Oversoul Seven

DAY 304

We can easily forgive a child who is afraid of the dark; the real tragedy of life is when men are afraid of the light.

—PLATO

DAY 305

A psychology that can lead us to encounter the mysteries must be rooted in an earth-based spirituality that knows the sacred—whether we name it Goddess, God, spirit or something else—is not outside the world, but manifests in nature, in human beings, in the community and culture we create. Every being is sacred—meaning that each has inherent value that cannot be ranked in a hierarchy or compared to the value of another being. Worth does not have to be earned, acquired or proven; it is inherent in our existence.

—STARHAWK
Truth or Dare

DAY 306

Religion is the realization of the true.

—BUDDHA

DAY 307

We make boundaries so that we can feel separate and move coherently through the world: it's part of our necessary natural growth to do that. In doing it, we forget the secret, which is that we are not separate. . . .

Respect your limits. Love your limits; they protect you from an abundance so immense it can be intolerable. If, however, you stretch your limits also, you will move in the direction of receiving and becoming unconditional love.

—JULIE HENDERSON
The Lover Within

DAY 308

The supreme happiness of life is the conviction
that we are loved.

—VICTOR HUGO

DAY 309

It is a rare privilege
to be born as a human being, as
we happen to be;
If we do not achieve enlightenment in this life,
when do we expect to achieve it?

—ECHU (Zen Poet)

DAY 310

We should . . . be aware at all times of the unique opportunity afforded by a human rebirth, so that we do not waste that opportunity. Our human existence is better than that of a cat or a dog, for a human being knows how to think and how to use and understand language. A human being also has a far greater capacity for doing evil in this world than do cats and dogs, as for example, the creating of nuclear weapons. But human beings also have the capacity to realize enlightenment in this life and thus their capacity is far superior to those of animals. This is the true significance of a human existence—our potential. Being aware of our real condition, both our limitations and our capacities, is what we mean by mindfulness and awareness.

—NAMKHAI NORBU
The Cycle of Day and Night

DAY 311

Man is certainly stark mad; he cannot make a worm, and yet he will be making gods by dozens.

—MONTAIGNE

DAY 312

The only faith that endures with man springs from heavenly love. Those without love have knowledge merely, or persuasion. Just to believe in truth and in the Word is not faith. Faith is to love truth, and to will and do it from inward affection for it.

—EMANUEL SWEDENBORG

DAY 313

Working the Mother (Goddess) is a job! It is a commitment to cultivate your intuitive faculties. It demands that you let go of old biases, old fears. It means recognizing and embracing those "others" who truly are your kindred spirits. It carries the responsibility of transforming your environment.

—LUISAH TEISH
Jambalaya: The Natural Woman's Book of Personal Charms and Practical Rituals

DAY 314

We each have an infinite supply of love and happiness within us. We have been accustomed to thinking we have to get something from the outside in order to be happy, but in truth it works the other way: we must learn to contact our inner source of happiness and satisfaction and flow it outward to share with others—not because it is virtuous to do so, but because it feels really good! Once we tune into it we just naturally want to share it because that is the essential nature of love, and we are all loving beings.

—SHAKTI GAWAIN
Creative Visualization

DAY 315

Man alone of all the creatures of earth can change his own pattern. Man alone is the architect of his own destiny.

—WILLIAM JAMES

DAY 316

The force of a thought is not an illusion. And the thought will never accept any contradiction. Thought dwells free. Like it wants to on the wings of an angel. It is quite simple. We must take the risk and act. It is the only proof that we have that we are. Creation needs to consider the future. Therefore, we cannot live unless we can see the future. It is true that we live each day, but today is only the present. We must englobe equally the future.

—ALEX TANNOUS
Reflexions sur la Vie Interieure

DAY 317

One person with a belief is equal to a force of ninety-nine who have only interest.

—JOHN STUART MILL

DAY 318

Therefore, leave all outer knowledge gained through the senses; do not work with the senses at all, either objectively or subjectively. For if those who mean to become contemplative, spiritual and inward-looking, reckon they ought to hear, smell, see, taste or feel spiritual things in external visions or in the depth of their being, they are seriously misled, and are working against the natural order of things. For the natural order is that by the senses we should gain our knowledge of the outward, material world, but not thereby acquire our knowledge of things spiritual.

—The Cloud of Unknowing

DAY 319

A small boy, upon being asked how he would describe God, said simply, "I think of Him as Light." Looked at from the angle of color and its places in our lives, this is a very apt description, for all life is energy vibrating at a different rate. Each vibration has a corresponding color and all color rays emanate from the central source, the Great White Light or Logos as we are instructed by the Ancient Teachings. In fact, as with everything else in life, there is an outer form to be perceived by our senses and an inner or hidden meaning to be discovered.

—MARY ANDERSON
Color Healing

DAY 320

Up from Earth's center through the Seventh gate
I rose, and on the Throne of Saturn sate,
And many a knot unraveled by the road,
But not the master-knot of human fate.
There was the Door to which I found no key;
There was the Veil through which I could not see;
Some little talk awhile of Thee and me
There was—and then no more of me and Thee.

—OMAR KHAYYAM

DAY 321

What is the meaning of human life, or for that matter of the life of any creature? To know the answer to this question means to be religious. You ask: Does it make any sense, then, to pose this question? I answer: The man who regards his own life and that of his fellow creatures as meaningless is not merely unhappy but hardly fit for life.

—ALBERT EINSTEIN

DAY 322

Let us be silent, that we may hear the whispers of
the gods.

—EMERSON

DAY 323

Love your life, poor as it is. You may perhaps
have some pleasant, thrilling, glorious hours, even
in a poorhouse. The setting sun is reflected from
the windows of the almshouse as brightly as from
the rich man's abode.

—THOREAU

DAY 324

Esoteric mysteries must be approached cautiously, with reverence and compassion, with a genuine desire to use their magics to end the world's suffering . . . to relieve the pain of individuals . . . and to bring happiness to friends and strangers alike. Yes, and also to enemies. Even especially to these. Then it will follow that joy and happiness will likewise descend upon its user in abundance. Endless miracles will manifest when love and peace rule in the heart of the one who has mastered the arts and sciences of ancient wisdom with goodwill and loving intent.

—LINDA GOODMAN
Linda Goodman's Star Signs

DAY 325

Those who have the strength and the love to sit with a dying patient in the *silence that goes beyond words* will know that this moment is neither frightening nor painful, but a peaceful cessation of the functioning of the body. Watching a peaceful death of a human being reminds us of a falling star; one of the million lights in a vast sky that flares up for a brief moment only to disappear into the endless night forever. To be a therapist to a dying patient makes us aware of the uniqueness of each individual in this vast sea of humanity. It makes us aware of our finiteness, our limited lifespan. Few of us live beyond our three score and ten years and yet in that brief time most of us create and live a unique biography and weave ourselves into the fabric of human history.

—ELISABETH KÜBLER-ROSS
On Death and Dying

DAY 326

A vague suspicion in the breast
That to begin implies to end.

—TENNYSON

DAY 327

Our birth is but a sleep and a forgetting;
The Soul that rises with us, our life's Star,
Hath had elsewhere its setting,
  And cometh from afar.

Not in entire forgetfulness
And not in utter nakedness
But trailing clouds of glory do we come
  From God, who is our home.

—WORDSWORTH

DAY 328

Matter is the vehicle for the manifestation of Soul on this plane of existence, and Soul is the vehicle on a higher plane for the existence of Spirit, and these three are a trinity synthesized by Life, which pervades them all.

—H. P. BLAVATSKY
The Secret Doctrine

DAY 329

Serenity is the end—and serenity is also the means—by which you live effectively. . . . The only reason you have not been happy every instant is that you have been dominating your consciousness with thoughts about something you don't have—or trying to hold onto something that you do have but which is no longer appropriate in the present flow of your life.

—KEN KEYES, JR.
Handbook to Higher Consciousness

DAY 330

If there is existence, there must be non-existence. And if there was a time when nothing existed, there must have been a time before that—when even nothing did not exist. Suddenly, when nothing came into existence, could one really say whether it belonged to the category of existence or non-existence?

—CHUANG-TZU

DAY 331

Who sees his Lord
Within every creature,
Deathlessly dwelling
Amidst the mortal:
That man sees truly.

—BHAGAVAD-GITA

DAY 332

The vision that you glorify in your mind, the ideal that you enthrone in your heart—this you will build your life by, this you will become.

—JAMES ALLEN
As You Think

DAY 333

The human mind never framed an aphorism containing a more important truth than this one: "All seeming misfortunes are blessings in disguise." There is but one qualification necessary to render this an aphorism of universal validity; namely, one must have performed his whole duty on the premises. That is to say, if he does all that he can, honestly and honorably, to avert a threatened calamity, he will find that if he yields not to discouragement or despair when the catastrophe comes, it will invariably prove to have been a blessing. Seeming calamities are often the result of one's having mistaken his calling; and it frequently happens that the best part of one's lifetime is spent in a vain search for the work which the Lord gave him to do. But if courage is not lost, and his career is characterized by industry and integrity, he is sure to find it at last. He can then look back upon his past life and see cause to thank God for every seeming misfortune as fervently as for every season of prosperity; for he will then realize that each has constituted a step in the pathway leading to his true sphere of usefulness.

—THOMSON JAY HUDSON
The Evolution of the Soul

DAY 334

Finding myself to exist in the world, I believe I shall, in some shape or other, always exist.

—BENJAMIN FRANKLIN

DAY 335

The lesson of life is practically to generalize; to believe what the years and the centuries say against the hours; to resist the usurpation of particulars; to penetrate to their catholic sense.

—EMERSON

DAY 336

The birth and death of man's body are commonly considered to be the beginning and ending of man. But if it could be demonstrated scientifically that man is not merely a body but also a soul inhabiting a body; and that, further, this soul existed before birth and will continue to exist after death, the discovery would transform psychological science. It would be as if a shaft had been dropped from surface levels of soil to deep-lying strata of the earth; modern "depth" psychology would appear as superficial as a two-inch hole for the planting of an onion by comparison with a two-mile shaft for the extraction of oil.

—EDGAR CAYCE

DAY 337

There is no here, no there. Infinity lies before our eyes.

—SENGTSAN
The Book of Angelus Silesius

DAY 338

The legend of Atlantis, now becoming a recognizable reality, is of importance to our modern world. Less than half a century ago it would have seemed incredible that mankind would be able effectively to destroy the human race and perhaps the planet itself. Nevertheless, this is the immediate possibility that we face from moment to moment. The possibility that a general catastrophe occurred thousands of years in the past through thermonuclear explosion or other discovery and eventual misuse of the force latent in the Earth is supported by myths and legends from all over the world and also by geophysical evidence from the land and, notably, from the sea. . . .

Increasing knowledge of the reality and the fate of Atlantis, even if it means reassessing the beginnings of history, may have the effect of bringing the peoples of the world together spiritually, because our common cultural roots in the civilization of the Eighth Continent, and intellectually, as it becomes more evident year by year and almost week by week that if the world does not soon attain a reasonable unity, it will destroy itself. Perhaps the memory and knowledge of an earlier world, as we learn more about it and what happened to it, can contribute to the preservation of the present world—a final contribution to its descendants from the ancient Empire of the Sea.

—CHARLES BERLITZ
Atlantis

DAY 339

All are but parts of one stupendous whole,
Whose body Nature is, and God the soul.

—ALEXANDER POPE

DAY 340

The name "heroes" is only a slight alteration of Eros, from whom the heroes sprang.

—PLATO

DAY 341

He who knows much about others may be learned, but he who understands himself is more intelligent. He who controls others may be powerful, but he who has mastered himself is mightier still.

—LAO TZU

DAY 342

Death is simply a shedding of the physical body, like a butterfly coming out of a cocoon. It is a transition into a higher state of consciousness, where you continue to perceive, to understand, to laugh, to be able to grow, and the only thing you lose is something that you don't need anymore, and that is your physical body.

—ELISABETH KÜBLER-ROSS
in *The World Beyond Death*

DAY 343

Man is immortal and the body cannot die, because matter has no life to surrender. The human concept named matter, death, disease, sickness and sin are all that can be destroyed. Death is but another phase of the dream that existence can be material.

—MARY BAKER EDDY

DAY 344

The world of birth and rebirth is like a dream, full of desires and hates; in its own time it shines as real, but on waking it becomes unreal.

—SHANKARA ACHARYA'S ATMA BODHA

DAY 345

For certain is death for the born, and certain is birth for the dead; therefore over the inevitable thou shouldst not grieve.

—BHAGAVAD-GITA

DAY 346

Enlightenment is not an attainment; it is a realization. And when you wake up, everything changes and nothing changes. If a blind man realizes that he can see, has the world changed?

—DAN MILLMAN
Way of the Peaceful Warrior

DAY 347

Dreams are perhaps the ultimate personal creation; for most of us they come from a part so deep within that even we, our conscious selves, have little control over them. But dreams are also the door, the flying carpet if you will, that can lead us to the untapped truths and possibilities that lie within us.

—JILL MORRIS
The Dream Workbook

DAY 348

Dreams are the touchstones of our characters.

—THOREAU

DAY 349

When, in an altered state of consciousness, a person relives what may be a past life, he is able to release fully his emotions and is able to accept responsibility for an action which he considers already performed and done with in another lifetime. Once the subject has made the transfer of responsibility to the present life experience and has recognized that the "fault" lies in a time far removed from current considerations, he is able to deal with the matter without embarrassment or shame.

Whether or not past-life awareness truly provides one with a working knowledge of the world beyond death will perhaps always remain a matter of individual assessment, but we have found that such awareness yields so many wonderful by-products. All the pleasures which are derived through the senses are enhanced. Sight, hearing, touch, smell, taste all become keener. One becomes capable of detecting subtleties which he has never before noticed. One gains a greater control of life and himself. Such self-mastery, such personal enrichment, enables one to transform his entire life into one that is fulfilling, pleasurable and happy. If it is not the world beyond death of which one gains knowledge, past-life awareness permits one to achieve deeper insights into the world beyond self, as well as the world within oneself. And again, one must ask if all three worlds may not blend in ways which will become immediately apparent at the moment of one's physical transition.

—BRAD STEIGER
The World Beyond Death

DAY 350

Ultimate insights have a tendency to undermine the orthodox approaches by which they have been reached.

—SANTAYANA

DAY 351

For this is the journey that men make: to find themselves. If they fail in this, it doesn't matter much else what they find.

—JAMES A. MICHENER

DAY 352

One reads of the "wounded healer," the person who learns from pain the end of pain and a connectedness with all others in similar discomfort. Spinal discomfort has taught me something of the reintegration of the heart which seems constantly to be reflected in the body, a softening around pain, an investigation of the incessant resistance and despair manifest in the desire to escape. In the first year of the spinal pain, bargaining with my discomfort, seeking healing techniques that might relieve me, like throwing meat to a rabid dog in order to keep him at bay a moment longer, hardly investigating that which intensified the disagreeableness of the experience, I went to see one of my teachers to ask how I might get rid of the pain. But instead of buying into my escape mechanisms, he said, "Don't look for relief, look for the truth!" This sentence has done more to propel our investigation than any other that comes to mind at this moment.

We are all wounded healers on the way to completion, entering our wholeness just beneath the surface of our superficial holdings. The investigation of discomfort leading us to a sense of satisfaction and wholeness we never imagined possible. Living in the lab, life becomes an experiment in truth.

—STEPHEN LEVINE
Healing into Life and Death

DAY 353

A vital aspect of the enlightened state is the experience of an all-pervading unity. "This" and "that" no longer are separate entities. They are different *forms* of the same thing. Everything is a *manifestation*. It is not possible to answer the question "Manifestation of *what*?" because the *what* is that which is beyond words, beyond concept, beyond form, beyond even space and time. Everything is a manifestation of that which is. That which is, is. Beyond these words lies the experience: the experience of that which is.

The forms through which that which is manifests itself are each and every one of them perfect. *We* are manifestations of that which is. Everything and everybody is exactly and perfectly what it is.

—GARY ZUKAV
The Dancing Wu Li Masters

DAY 354

Consult the dead upon the things that were,
But the living only on things that are.

—LONGFELLOW

DAY 355

We know that the wistful eyes of Life are set toward a vision that is also a Home—a Home from which news can reach us now and again. Thus, looking out from ourselves to our Universe, we seem to catch a glimpse of something behind that great pictorial cosmos of suns and systems of suns, that more immediate world of struggle, death and decay, which intellect has disentangled from the Abyss. The greater man's mental detachment from the mere struggle to live, which forces him to select, label and dwell upon the useful aspects of things, the more chance there is that we may obtain from him some account of the meaning of that struggle and the aim of the Spirit of Life.

—EVELYN UNDERHILL
The Mystic Way

DAY 356

If you refuse to accept anything but the best out of life, you very often get it.

—W. SOMERSET MAUGHAM

DAY 357

In love, the Horned God, changing form and changing face, ever seeks the Goddess. In this world, the search and the seeking appear in the Wheel of the Year.

She is the Great Mother who gives birth to Him as the Divine child Sun at the Winter Solstice. In spring, He is sower and seed who grows with the growing light, green as the new shoots. She is the Initiatrix who teaches Him the mysteries. He is the young bull; She the nymph, seductress. In summer, when light is longest, they meet in union, and the strength of their passion sustains the world. But the God's face darkens as the sun grows weaker, until at last, when the grain is cut for harvest, He too sacrifices Himself to Self that all may be nourished. She is the reaper, the grave of earth to which all must return. Throughout the long nights and darkening days, He sleeps in her womb, in dreams. He is Lord of Death who rules the Land of Youth beyond the gates of night and day. His dark tomb becomes the womb of rebirth, for at Midwinter She again gives birth to Him. The cycle ends and begins again and the Wheel of the Year turns on and on.

—STARHAWK
The Spiral Dance

DAY 358

It is one thing to know truths, another to acknowledge them, and yet another to have faith in them. Only the faithful can have faith.

—EMANUEL SWEDENBORG

DAY 359

All nature is art, unknown to thee;
All chance, direction, which thou canst not see;
All discord, harmony, not understood.
All partial evil, Universal Good;
And, spite of pride, in erring reason's spite,
One truth is clear, Whatever is, is right.

—POPE

DAY 360

If one advances confidently in the direction of his dreams, and endeavors to live the life which he has imagined, he will meet with a success unexpected in common hours.

—THOREAU

DAY 361

To lose the chance to see frigate birds soaring in circles above the storm, or a file of pelicans winging their way homeward across the crimson afterglow of the sunset, or a myriad terns flashing in the bright light of midday as they hover in a shifting maze above the beach—why, the loss is like the loss of a gallery of the masterpieces of the artists of old time.

—THEODORE ROOSEVELT

DAY 362

Do you want to know more about extraterrestrials? Do you want a definition of angels? We are you yourself in the distant past and distant future. We are you as you were, would have been and still are, had you not fallen from your original state of grace. We exist in a parallel universe of non-form, experiencing what you would have experienced had you not become associated with the materializing processes. I act in this capacity as a midwife at your birth into form. I am an angel of destiny, a messenger from the stars, but I am also the reflection of your unity before and after matter. I am here to enter your consciousness, here to wake you up.

—KEN CAREY
The Starseed Transmissions

DAY 363

Immortal memory never dies, but lives
Forever in the highest realms of being,
And like seeks like through all the universe.

—RUFUS C. HOPKINS
in *The Metaphysical Magazine*, 1895

DAY 364

The key to our flowering at this final stage of our evolutionary cycle lies in the simplicity of being in resonance. Even more, it is through remaining in resonance that the solar-psychic frequency, mediated by the terrestrial electromagnetic battery, is maintained; that the light body is nourished; and that we may discover the knowledge and energy necessary for our own individual maintenance. To say that we are knocking on the doors of magic is only to acknowledge our own lack of belief in what we are actually capable of through our own instrumentation, the sensory body. What has been demonstrated by shamans and wizards, yogis and spiritual masters, is—after all—everyone's evolutionary birthright.

—JOSE ARGUELLES
The Mayan Factor

DAY 365

Ultimately, your greatest teacher
is to live with an open heart.

—EMMANUEL

ACKNOWLEDGMENTS

Material from *As You Think* by James Allen, updated by Marc Allen, 1987. Reprinted by permission of Whatever Publishing, Inc.

Material from *Color Healing* by Mary Anderson. Copyright © 1985 by Mary Anderson. Reprinted by permission of Thorsons Publishing Group Ltd.

Material from *Jaguar Woman* by Lynn Andrews. Copyright © 1985 by Lynn Andrews. Reprinted by permission of Harper & Row, Publishers, Inc.

Material from *The Mayan Factor* by Jose Arguelles. Copyright © 1987 by Jose Arguelles, published by Bear & Company, P.O. Drawer 2860, Santa Fe, New Mexico 87504.

Material from *Jonathan Livingston Seagull* by Richard Bach. Copyright © 1970 by Richard D. Bach and Leslie Parrish Bach. Reprinted by permission of Macmillan Publishing Company.

Material from *Windows of Light* by Randall N. Baer and Vicki V. Baer. Copyright © 1984 by Randall N. Baer and Vicki V. Baer. Reprinted by permission of Harper and Row, Publishers, Inc.

Material from *Music and Sound in the Healing Arts* by John Beaulieu. Copyright © 1987 by John Beaulieu. Reprinted by permission of Station Hill Press, Barrytown, New York. All rights reserved.

Material from *Atlantis—The Eighth Continent* by Charles Berlitz. Copyright © 1984 by Charles Berlitz. Reprinted by permission of the Putnam Publishing Group.

Material from *The Cosmic Crystal Spiral* by Ra Bonewitz. Copyright © 1986 by Ra Bonewitz. Reprinted by permission of Element Books, Ltd., Shaftesbury, Dorset, Great Britain.